Mind and Body

Central Problems of Philosophy

Series Editor: John Shand

This series of books presents concise, clear, and rigorous analyses of the core problems that preoccupy philosophers across all approaches to the discipline. Each book encapsulates the essential arguments and debates, providing an authoritative guide to the subject while also introducing original perspectives. This series of books by an international team of authors aims to cover those fundamental topics that, taken together, constitute the full breadth of philosophy.

Published titles

Causation and Explanation
Stathis Psillos

Free Will
Graham McFee

Knowledge
Michael Welbourne

Meaning
David E. Cooper

Mind and Body
Robert Kirk

Ontology
Dale Jacquette

Perception
Barry Maund

Relativism
Paul O'Grady

Scepticism
Neil Gascoigne

Truth
Pascal Engel

Universals
J. P. Moreland

Forthcoming titles

Action
Rowland Stout

Modality
Joseph Melia

Paradox
Doris Olin

Philosophy and Science
James Logue

Realism and Anti-Realism
Stuart Brock & Edwin Mares

Self
Stephen Burwood

Value
Chris Cherry

Mind and Body

Robert Kirk

First published in 2003 by Acumen

Acumen Publishing Limited
15a Lewins Yard
East Street
Chesham
Bucks HP5 1HQ
www.acumenpublishing.co.uk

ISBN: 1-902683-79-X (hardcover)
ISBN: 1-902683-80-3 (paperback)

British Library Cataloguing-in-Publication Data
A catalogue record for this book is available from
the British Library.

Designed and typeset by Kate Williams, Abergavenny.
Printed and bound by Biddles Ltd., Guildford and King's Lynn.

Contents

Preface

This is an introduction to the mind–body problem – a complex tangle. No previous knowledge of the subject-matter is presupposed, but the reader with a year or two's acquaintance with philosophy will probably benefit most. The aim is to provide insights into what's puzzling about the main problems, what's important in the main theories, and what's good or bad about (some of) the main arguments. Since much contemporary philosophy is devoted to issues in this area, it would not have been sensible in a short work to have attempted to cover either all relevant topics or all important contributions. Instead I have tried to provide a compact, reliable framework that holds the reader's interest, and which can be built on as needed. I have also tried to encourage a questioning approach: switching between "sponge" and "rapier" modes makes reading philosophy more fun. There are suggestions for further reading at the end of each chapter, and full references at the end, where one or two useful websites are listed.

My thanks to colleagues and generations of students whose penetrating and often disconcerting questions over the years have stimulated my thinking. Thanks to two readers for Acumen for useful comments and suggestions. Thanks also to my wife Janet for all kinds of help.

Introduction: are we
1 just machines?

1.1 Clockwork Snoopy

Here is a wind-up toy dog, Snoopy, about as big as my thumb. He stands on two legs, and when I wind him up the clockwork motor makes his legs move and he walks. When he hits an obstacle he sometimes stops, sometimes rocks gently and moves off in a different direction. If you were very simple-minded you might think Snoopy *decided* to stop walking, then decided to move off again; and that generally he knew what he was doing. But we know this clockwork toy really has no thoughts or feelings.

Why are we so confident? Do we know what it takes to have thoughts and feelings? Plenty of philosophers would say we do, but plenty would disagree. As a preliminary to studying the mind–body problem it will be useful to consider the following question:

What reasons are there for thinking that the clockwork dog has neither thoughts nor feelings?

Here are some of the replies people typically offer:

A. It isn't conscious.
B. It hasn't got a mind (or a soul).
C. It hasn't got a brain.
D. It's just a machine.
E. It's made of the wrong stuff.
F. It doesn't behave in the right ways.

Discussing these suggestions will help to expose some main strands in the complex tangle of the mind–body problem.

1.2 Why doesn't the clockwork dog have thoughts or feelings?

Reply A: "It isn't conscious."
That is surely true. However, plenty of people accept that we have unconscious thoughts; and some philosophers argue there can be unconscious experiences too. So even though it seems clear that clockwork Snoopy isn't conscious, that doesn't settle the matter. Besides, to say it isn't conscious immediately raises the question of how we know. The answers tend to be like the ones given to the first question, so we're not much further forward.

Reply B: "It hasn't got a mind or a soul."
You might object that minds and souls are very different kinds of thing, not to be lumped together. But whatever exactly may be meant by those words, it seems clear that clockwork Snoopy has neither. Unfortunately this too doesn't seem to move us forward. Consider what is supposed to be involved in having a mind or a soul. Many who take the idea seriously will agree that the whole point of having one is that it enables you to have thoughts and feelings. If that is right, the present suggestion amounts to no more than saying that the clockwork dog lacks thoughts and feelings because it lacks whatever would have enabled it to have thoughts or feelings.

Reply C: "It hasn't got a brain."
When someone tells Scarecrow in *The Wizard of Oz* to make up his mind, he tells them "I haven't got a brain, only straw. So I haven't got a mind to make up." Cogent reasoning – assuming a brain is necessary for having a mind. Is it?

We know that with us and other terrestrial animals the brain is heavily involved in the control of behaviour. But perhaps things could have been different. Perhaps robotic systems or alien organisms could be adequately controlled in some different way, without brains. It's one thing to say a very simple system like clockwork Snoopy has no thoughts or feelings; something else to say no possible robot or computer-controlled system whatever could have them. If it could, then brains are not necessary for thinking and feeling.

Reply D: "It's just a machine."
Of course the machines we are familiar with don't even seem capable of having thoughts or feelings. But that doesn't mean no machine at all could have thoughts or feelings. Many scientists and philosophers claim it might eventually become possible to construct sophisticated robots with genuine intelligence and even consciousness.

It's also true that clockwork Snoopy isn't *alive*. But we know that being alive is not *sufficient* for having thoughts or feelings (unless we happen to believe that even plants can feel). If sophisticated robots can be intelligent, it isn't necessary either.

Reply E: "It's made of the wrong stuff."
We are strongly inclined to suppose that nothing made of plastic and metal could have thoughts or feelings. But why not? Two reasons for challenging this reply can be noted straight away. First, if you inspect a brain, living or dead, it looks an unpromising source of thoughts and feelings. If there has to be one bodily organ to do the job, then perhaps, as the ancients supposed, the heart is the more promising candidate. We can at least feel it beating; and loud insistent heartbeats signify strong emotion. Regardless of whether we choose the heart or the brain, though, there seems to be a huge gap between the physiological facts about those organs on the one hand, and thoughts and feelings on the other. The inclination to say that plastic and metal are not the right sort of stuff could turn out to be prejudice. What do brains have that metal and plastic lack?

You might suggest that brains can *do* things that plastic and metal can't. That's true: for one thing, brains bleed. But so what? Evidently the question has to be whether plastic and metal can do the *right kinds* of things. Perhaps further advances in technology will enable them to do what brains can do. Even today bits of plastic and metal can be inserted into people's heads to take over some functions of the inner ear. Why shouldn't it be possible to have totally synthetic brains? Perhaps the trouble is not that the stuff is the wrong kind, but that the mechanisms are the wrong kind. If so, again we meet a further question: what makes the difference between right and wrong kinds of mechanism?

Many people find it so mysterious that anything material should have thoughts or feelings that they think something extra must be involved, something beyond the merely physical. That idea, which arose in very ancient times and is still influential, no doubt partly helps to explain the persistence of the mind–body problem.

It is not the whole of the explanation. Even if we are purely physical organisms and nothing beyond the physical is involved in thoughts and feelings, that leaves most of the main philosophical problems still unsolved, as we shall see.

Reply F: "It doesn't behave in the right ways."
Clockwork Snoopy has a very limited behavioural repertoire, while human beings seem capable of indefinitely many different types of behaviour. That is particularly clear when we consider language. We are able to understand an indefinitely large number of sentences, and similarly we can construct and produce an indefinitely large number of sentences, which others can understand. Clockwork Snoopy has nothing approaching those capacities. But that still doesn't settle the matter. After all, young infants and dumb animals have no language to speak of, and generally a very restricted behavioural repertoire. Why shouldn't clockwork Snoopy have a limited repertoire of thoughts and feelings to go with its limited behavioural repertoire, rather than none at all?

You might think the point is not so much that clockwork Snoopy can't do *enough*, as that he can't do the right sorts of things. But what are they? What sorts of behaviour, if any, reveal that the system (organism, robot, Martian, whatever) is a genuine subject of thoughts and feelings, not just a clever mimic? That question becomes especially urgent if linguistic behaviour is not necessary.

1.3 Going deeper

You may have been getting impatient with the replies I have discussed so far. You will probably be sympathetic to the last one, but point out that the main trouble with Snoopy is not so much that he doesn't do the right sorts of things as that he is (a) insensitive to the world around him, and (b) lacks the ability to work out fresh ways of behaving. If observing his actual behaviour isn't enough to convince us of (a) and (b), then studying his insides will clinch the matter. There is only a simple clockwork motor, whose cogwheels turn a cam which lifts Snoopy's legs one after the other. Nothing else; and in particular, no mechanisms for receiving information from the outside world, and none for processing that information and working out appropriate behaviour.

It is at least highly plausible that unless an organism or an artificial behaving system is sensitive to the world outside it, and also able to work out fresh ways of behaving, it can't qualify as having thoughts or feelings. (I say only that this is "highly plausible" because some people maintain there could be thoughts and feelings in a thing without those seemingly vital features.)

Mentioning Snoopy's insides reminds us that although a great deal is still not known about the detailed workings of human and animal brains and nervous systems, a great deal has already been discovered, and more is being discovered every day. In spite of the enormous difficulty of the task it might eventually be successfully completed, in the sense that scientists will thoroughly understand how the brain and central nervous system generally function. Will the philosophical problems thereby be solved? Some influential philosophers think so: Daniel Dennett, for example (see his *Consciousness Explained*, 1991). However, even if that is correct, it is far from obvious.

One reason is that discovering the workings of animal bodies and nervous systems will not automatically tell us *which features of these systems matter* from the point of view of an interest in the nature of thinking and feeling in general. It will not automatically enable us to tell whether a complicated robot – which we can take to be any system controlled by a standard type of computer – has thoughts or feelings, for example. Nor will it automatically enable us to decide whether *all* that matters is how the system behaves, as some philosophers – philosophical "behaviourists" – still maintain ("If it looks like a duck, flies like a duck, walks like a duck, and quacks like a duck, it's a duck"). The scientists themselves discuss such questions – but by doing so they engage in philosophy.

Yet if science alone won't solve all the problems, philosophy alone isn't going to do it either. Some of the philosophical problems arise only because of our acquaintance with scientific and technological achievements. An example is provided by the work of Ludwig Wittgenstein, who died in 1952. Although research in artificial intelligence had started before Wittgenstein stopped working, and although Alan Turing had already published a significant non-technical paper on these matters in 1950, developments in computing were very far from the stage they have reached today. Those developments in both hardware and software raise possibilities which Wittgenstein just did not consider, as we shall see later in this chapter and in Chapters 5 and 7.

1.4 Consciousness, intentionality and explanation

There is no single clearly defined "mind–body problem". As the examples of the toy dog and the sophisticated robot suggest, we face a complex of interrelated problems and puzzles. But the following double question will serve as a brisk statement of the problem:

(a) What is it to have thoughts and feelings? and
(b) how are thoughts and feelings related to the physical world?

You might reckon we could leave out (a); but surely we can't hope to understand how thoughts and feelings are related to the physical world unless we have some understanding of the nature of thoughts and feelings themselves.

I take *feelings* to include sensations, emotions and perceptions; I will also use "consciousness" to cover this large aspect of mental life. Experiences, feelings, emotions and the like have "subjective character": there is *something it is like* to have them. This feature is sometimes called "phenomenal consciousness". We want to know what it is for something to be phenomenally conscious. Can a purely physical system (organism, artefact, extraterrestrial) be phenomenally conscious? How can a mere mound of molecules have mentality? We shall be constantly returning to these questions; they will receive extended treatment in Chapter 8.

The particularly problematic feature of *thinking* is "intentionality". This is the technical-sounding word standardly applied to that feature of our thoughts by which they can be *about* things, and in some cases true or false. (Note that intentionality is not confined to intentions.) Can a purely physical system have intentionality? How is that possible? Again, we shall be considering this and related questions throughout, with an extended treatment in Chapter 7.

There are some reasons to suppose that thinking and feeling are fundamentally different; but many philosophers argue that they are different sides of the same coin. Further, our problems are not just a result of the fact that the things physics tells us about seem very different from thoughts and feelings. The *explanations* offered by physics are in several ways unlike those offered by psychology. The relations between physical and psychological explanations will be discussed at several points in the course of the book; I will draw some of the threads together in Chapter 9.

Intentionality, consciousness, their relations, and relations between physical and psychological explanations: these, then, are the main components of the "mind–body problem".

1.5 Exploring possibilities

Snoopy is a machine without either thoughts or feelings. But we can agree on that (assuming we do agree) largely because it is such a very simple machine. What about a more complex system, such as a computer-controlled robot? The question of whether such a thing could have thoughts or feelings has come up already. I will pursue it in the rest of this chapter, since although it may not be the most usual way to introduce the mind–body problem, it offers an interesting route to some important ideas and further questions. I will focus on John Searle's famous "Chinese Room" argument which shows, he thinks, that no robot (that is, no computer-controlled system) could *possibly* understand Chinese or anything else. However, possibility, impossibility and necessity – *modality* for short – are well-known sources of philosophical difficulty; we need to have some idea why and how it seems necessary (!) to use these concepts in our investigations.

Searle is not trying to show only that a robot with genuine understanding is not *practically* possible. Those who oppose his views on the matter don't have to come up with an actual Chinese-speaking robot. What they claim, and Searle disputes, is that there are no *theoretical* obstacles to the existence of such a robot. Their claim could be true even if the task of actually designing and constructing one proved to be practically impossible not just at present, or in the next few decades, but forever. For the same reason Searle is not trying to show that such a robot is impossible in another way: that it would involve some conflict with the laws of nature, or is "nomologically" impossible; although of course that would be extremely interesting if true.

One way of describing Searle's aim is to say he is trying to show that such a robot is not even *logically* possible. Unfortunately this expression is controversial as well as vague. Yet it remains useful for roughly marking a supposed distinction between possibilities that are ruled out by practical or merely physical factors, and those that are ruled out because they either make no sense or somehow involve a contradiction. For our purposes we can take it that something is *logically impossible* if and only if its description entails a contradiction or is in some other way "incoherent" (another regrettably vague expression).

In order to show that a robot with genuine understanding is not even logically possible Searle uses a "thought-experiment". A thought-experiment describes a state of affairs that is for some reason difficult to set up in reality, and is intended to throw fresh light on what is possible or actual. In one highly influential thought-experiment Descartes invites us to imagine that a powerful and malicious demon is causing him to have all the experiences which he takes to be perceptions of a real external world, and that those experiences are nothing but illusions. (See his *First Meditation*, where he is presenting his method for finding certainty in the teeth of scepticism.) Thought experiments are not confined to philosophy, by the way: Schrödinger's cat is one well-known scientific thought-experiment.

When considering a thought-experiment in philosophy we need to be specially on guard against the possibility that it is just a device for reinforcing prejudices – which Daniel Dennett calls an "intuition pump". One test is whether the argument supposedly backed up by the thought-experiment can also be presented in straightforward literal terms; for although some thought-experiments are indeed no more than devices for reinforcing prejudices, others help to make philosophical points vivid even though they can be perfectly well defended without them. (Kripke's example of God creating the physical universe is an example: see §2.7.)

We are interested in the "nature" of thoughts and feelings. However, the concept of a thing's nature is another vague but seemingly indispensable one. In ordinary conversation it doesn't usually bother us. When considering artefacts such as tables or watches or computers, we can usually answer questions about their nature by mentioning their *functions*. If their functions are already known, then explaining how they are designed, and perhaps how they are constructed, will be enough. When it comes to the natural world we can appeal to evolution and the idea of natural functions (such as the heart's function of pumping blood); we can also explain how biological systems such as plants or animals work, and what they are made of; and we can explain the processes at work in the inanimate world (formation of stars and planets, movements of tectonic plates, or whatever). But matters are not so straight-forward when we enquire philosophically about the nature of thinking and feeling.

Purely scientific accounts of the processes involved in thinking and feeling, to the extent that they are available, are of course extremely valuable. But knowing what goes on in the bodies and brains of actual organisms will not automatically explain what thinking and feeling *are*; it will not automatically explain what *matters* about the processes explained.

Some philosophers are sceptical about the assumptions behind such questions. Don't they presuppose that there are "essences"? (Roughly, a thing's essence is, or would be, whatever it could not fail to have without ceasing to exist.) Both Wittgenstein and Quine, in very different ways, have taught us to be wary of such assump-tions. However, even if we are not justified in assuming there are essences, we can still try to find out what it is about something on account of which it qualifies as a subject of thinking or feeling; and that will be part of our task.

1.6 Mechanism

The idea that human beings are machines is *mechanism*. If it is correct, the relation between the mental and the physical is a lot less mysterious than many people suppose. Showing how to construct a robot with real thoughts and feelings would therefore be a pretty convincing way to dispose of some of the central components of the mind–body problem. But is it even logically possible? Searle's Chinese Room argument at least appears to show that it is not. If he is right, we could not possibly be machines of the sorts exemplified by ordinary computers and robots. However, it is a striking fact that Searle accepts that we are machines of a different kind (see §1.12).

It will be useful to make sure we are reasonably clear about the main features of ordinary computers. (The next section may be skipped by those familiar with computers.)

1.7 Main features of standard computers

Consider an ordinary diary. It is a kind of information storage or *memory* system. It has a special place for each day, which we can find because we know the procedure for giving each day of the year its own individual date (in computer-speak, each location in the diary has its own "address"); in these places we can *write* information; we can *delete* information and *insert* different information; and we can *read* the information from any given place. Comparably a standard computer has a large "memory" with a number of "locations"; each location has its own "address"; information can be "written" into these memory locations, deleted, replaced and "read". The computer's memory consists of many tiny electronic circuits, each capable of one or other of two states corresponding to "0" and "1", the so-called binary digits or bits which are used to encode information inside the computer. (For example, each character on the standard keyboard has its own binary coding: the code for "A" might be "00000001"; for "a" it might be "00000010".)

While we have no trouble writing information directly into the diary, or reading from its pages, the computer needs a special *input unit* (usually a keyboard) and an *output unit* (usually a screen) for these purposes. But the key difference between the diary and the computer is this. While the diary's contents stay unchanged until we ourselves write or delete something, the computer has its own device for altering the contents of its memory as a result of instructions or *programs* also stored in its memory. It's a sort of super diary. If there were such a super diary, on some special pages labelled "instructions" you could write down whatever you wanted the diary to do, and the diary itself would execute your instructions. You might write down: "List any appointments I've got next week which are due to start before 10am." When you shut the diary it would produce the list.

A computer actually does just that sort of thing. The unit that does the work is the *arithmetic-logic unit* (ALU). It contains circuits such as the addition circuit which, when sequences of "0"s and "1"s representing numbers are fed into it, produces their sum. There is a code (a sequence of "0"s and "1"s) for each operation – the code for "add" might be "010", for example. There is also a formula in the computer's "machine code" for the address of each location in memory. So one of the lines of the computer's program might be "01011011011", and this might be "machine code" for the instruction: "Add the contents of location 1101 to the contents of location 1011 and replace the latter with the result." The "0"s and "1"s in the computer's machine code may be represented in the computer's hardware by, for example, high- and low-voltage impulses. Note that the sequences of high- and low-voltage impulses, or whatever else actually embodies the sequences of "0"s and "1"s, act directly on the electronic circuits in the ALU and immediately cause the specified operation to be performed. Another thing the ALU does is deal with conditional instructions, such as: "If the number in location 1001 is greater than 0, then go to the instruction in location 111, otherwise go to the next instruction."

Everything the computer does consists of operations of the limited kinds just mentioned. The ALU doesn't have to be able to perform more than a handful of arithmetical and other operations such as addition, because more complicated operations are broken down into that handful of very simple operations and, as everybody knows, it works extremely fast. When we use our personal computers in the ordinary way we are not aware of the machines' workings because we don't actually program computers in terms of "0"s and "1"s and elementary operations – in terms of their "machine codes". In fact most of us don't program our personal computers at all except in very indirect ways, via the menus in their operating systems, or in other software. The computer itself translates these "high-level" instructions into its own fundamental machine code.

To ensure that the impulses through the machine's complex system of interconnecting wires don't get muddled up, the computer has a timing device known as its *control unit* (a misleading name, since what actually controls its operations is the instructions or programs).

Stripped of distracting details, then, the main functional units of a standard computer are these:

(a) *memory*: lots of tiny on–off circuits;
(b) *ALU*, which performs the operations that are the vital working of the computer;
(c) *control unit*, timing the flow of signals through the whole system, including inputs and outputs;
(d) *input unit*;
(e) *output unit*.

See Figure 1, in which (a), (b) and (c) make up the *central processor* (CP). The boxes correspond to broad functions conceived very abstractly, not to physical components. Thick arrows represent data; thin arrows represent control signals.

Finally, notice that the computer will do absolutely nothing (apart from things like humming) unless it is running a program. Don't be misled by the fact that your own computer did things before you gave it any instructions: it came fitted with an "operating system", which is a sophisticated program. Just what a computer does depends on the nature of its program. If it is programmed to repeat the letter "a" until further notice, it won't make you think it is intelligent. If it is running a sophisticated chess program, on the other hand, it might make you think so.

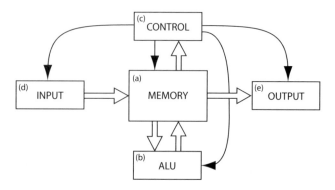

Figure 1

1.8 Computers and robots

Everyone knows that computers, suitably programmed, do all sorts of things that previously could be done only by human beings. For example, calculating the salary for each employee of a large firm; storing rail timetable information and producing routes with times and connections when given information about destinations and departure/arrival times; diagnosing medical conditions; playing chess. Since previously those things could be done only by human beings, we are easily led to describe what a computer does when running a sophisticated program in terms that earlier would have been applied only to human beings. "Diagnose", "predict" and "play" (as in a game) are verbs that seem to imply something like human performances. If we describe these machines as intelligent, are we misusing the word? Or are we literally correct? I hope what follows will provide a basis for sensible answers.

Let's restrict our use of the word "robot" to the sort of system you have when a suitably programmed computer is in control of a system which has (a) something like sense receptors (for example an array of light-sensitive cells and suitable connections from them to its controlling program), and (b) some sort of capacity for interacting with things outside it (for example an arm). Computers on their own can do all kinds of interesting things. But robots can do those things and a lot more, since they can "sense" and interact with the rest of the world in ways apparently more like the ways we and other animals do.

Some people have made very strong claims for what robots could in time be made to do. They don't generally make these claims for what has so far actually been produced; they are talking about what could eventually be produced. The following question focuses on a strong claim.

> Could a suitably programmed computer or robot eventually be made that would understand what was said to it, hold various beliefs, and make decisions?

Many people think that a computer-controlled robot, suitably programmed, *could* literally understand what was said to it, have various beliefs, make decisions, and have other mental states of the kinds we typically ascribe to one another – even if it might never become practical actually to construct such a thing. But here are some objections that people tend to raise, together with possible (not decisive) replies.

Objection 1   The very fact that a computer only does what it is programmed to do means it is completely without intelligence and therefore has no beliefs or other mental states of its own.

Reply 1   Newborn infants have a sort of program which enables them to learn how to move about, walk, talk and so on.

The objector may think this reply misses the point. A weighing machine, for example, is so constructed that each possible "input" to it – each possible weight placed on it – causes a certain fixed "output" (the reading for that weight, such as "2.25 kilos"). The machine doesn't understand what's going on – and nor, the objector thinks, does the computer. So we have a further objection:

Objection 2   That reply ignores the mechanical way the computer works. The programmers have anticipated each possible situation that the machine could be in – each possible pattern of stimulation of its "sense-receptors" – and they have ensured that when that pattern turns up, the machine puts out a certain fixed pattern of behaviour. So the thing can't possibly be described as intelligent.

Reply 2   That isn't even true for a pocket calculator, much less for a robot with a sophisticated program. When you key in 123 times 456 on your pocket calculator, and it gives 56,088 as the result, that is *not* because the makers anticipated that particular multiplication problem. All they did was to construct circuits that would work in accordance with the rules of arithmetic, enabling the system to deal with whatever was thrown at it. Similarly for the robot. The programmers give it something like rules governing its behaviour, but not specific instructions for each possible situation.

Objection 3   It would be impossible to devise a program to give the robot anything like human intelligence: the program would be vastly more complex than anything we could ever hope to produce.

Reply 3   The practical difficulties might indeed be insuperable. But even if they are, it doesn't follow that there couldn't *be* a suitable program. Perhaps a freak electrical storm might cause a robot's computer to be equipped with the right sort of program even if nobody could understand exactly how it worked. Or perhaps old-fashioned artificial intelligence (AI) enthusiasts were right after all, and we ourselves are organisms with the right sorts of programs.

Objection 4   A robot is made of the wrong stuff to have real thoughts, much less feelings.

Reply 4   We anticipated this sort of point when discussing Snoopy earlier (see reply E in §1.2). Why should it matter what the thing is made of?

When we program a computer we know what the sentences we key in mean. In a medical computer, for example, the doctors understand words like "protein" and "asthma". But does it follow that the machine itself understands them? Surely not. Hence another objection:

Objection 5   The machine is just a device we use to store and process our own information. The fact that it churns out expressions we understand doesn't imply it understands them itself. We may talk as if it understands them, but it doesn't.

Reply 5   That is true as far as it goes. No doubt the medical database cannot properly be said to understand the information in it. But it doesn't follow that a suitably programmed robot could not possibly understand what it said. We're talking about a robot that interacts with the world in ways rather like the ways we ourselves do. If we understand what we say to one another, that isn't magic. There must be an explanation. Why shouldn't that explanation, whatever it may be, apply to a suitably programmed robot?

1.9 Searle's Chinese Room argument

Searle lumps beliefs, desires, intentions and related states together as "cognitive states". In his own words, the view he is attacking is that "the appropriately programmed computer literally has cognitive states" (1980: 353. He calls his target "strong AI"). Properly

understood, his argument is quite general. If it works, it totally
. demolishes the idea that a computer could ever have genuine
understanding, even in the remote future. He aims to show that
such a thing is not possible at all.

Searle's argument depends on the fact that anything a computer
can do by running a program could also be done – given enough
time – by a human being following instructions in English. The
ability to understand Chinese exemplifies one kind of understanding. He invites us to suppose for the sake of argument that there
was a computer program which really succeeded in enabling the
computer to understand Chinese. He then imagines himself shut in
a room with a whole lot of instructions or rule books in English
which enable him to do by hand what the computer's program
supposedly enables it to do. When strings of Chinese characters are
posted through the letter-box, Searle deals with them in accordance
with his rule-books and puts out the results – which are also
sequences of Chinese characters.

It is not necessary to follow all the details of Searle's own presentation (especially not the details of the AI researcher Schank's
special notions of "scripts", "stories" and "questions": Searle 1980,
354ff.). Recall that a computer's central processor or CP consists of
its memory, its ALU and its control unit. The main steps of Searle's
argument can now be stated (though not in his own words) as
follows:

> Suppose C is a computer program which (if possible) enables a
> computer to understand Chinese, and C* is a set of rule-books
> in English which enables Searle to perform the same operations
> as C enables the computer to perform. It follows that if Searle
> is in a room acting in accordance with those rule-books C*,
> then when written Chinese is put through the letter-box, C*
> must enable him to put out acceptable responses in Chinese.
> Not only that: C* must enable the system to understand Chi-
> nese. However, since all the computer's CP does is to manipu-
> late what Searle calls "formal symbols" – they might as well be
> mere squiggles and totally meaningless – he too has only to
> manipulate formal symbols. He doesn't have to translate the
> Chinese characters into English. And he doesn't have to under-
> stand Chinese – nor does he. He concludes that because the

computer does essentially the same as he does, the computer doesn't understand Chinese either, in which case C cannot do what it was assumed to be able to do.

The following questions may help to clarify key points.

1. Is it an objection that the argument starts off with the assumption that the original computer program C actually does enable the computer to understand Chinese?

Searle's opponents claim there could eventually be a program which did what C is supposed to do; he is attempting to prove that there could not possibly be any such program. His argument is thus a "reductio ad absurdum". Suppose your obstinate friend insists that this path leads to the station and you want to prove it doesn't. One convincing method would be to *pretend* to accept that your friend is right, go together along the path – and show it takes you somewhere quite different. In effect Searle is saying to his opponents: "Let's pretend you're right. I'll show that even if we start from that assumption we can see it is after all mistaken."

2. Is Searle right to assume that if he doesn't have to understand Chinese in order to operate the rule-books C*, then the computer needn't understand Chinese either?

Answering this crucial question needs some care. Because merely shuffling the Chinese characters about in accordance with the rules won't enable *him* to understand Chinese, Searle assumes it won't enable the *computer* to understand Chinese either. For it's agreed on all sides that he is doing what matters about what the computer is doing. That gives rise to an intermediate question:

3. Is Searle right to assume that, no matter how long he goes on operating with the rule-books C*, it won't result in his learning Chinese?

The rule-books might include instructions like: "When squiggle-squiggle appears in the input sentence, follow instruction 234 in rule-book 56 and write down the result on page 333 of your notebook. Then go back and see if squoggle-squoggle appears in the sentence too. If it does, go to instruction 123 in book 45 and apply it to what you have just written on page 333; if it does not, go to instruction 67 in book 8 and write down the result on page 334 of your notebook." Instead of things like "squiggle-squiggle", of course, the rules will either have actual Chinese characters (which by hypothesis Searle doesn't understand) or binary codes (such as "10011010010").

The rules nowhere give any indications of how to *translate* Chinese expressions into English – obviously not, because they make no connections between Chinese expressions and objects. There is nothing like "Only use squoggle-squoggle when you're talking about rabbits", for instance. Such statements would have implied, falsely, that not only Searle but the *computer* knew what rabbits are, *independently* of the program. But that last remark raises a further question:

4. Does the central processor understand anything at all?

The CP may perhaps be said to "understand" the very small set of binary coded instructions which (in §1.7) we noted are what cause the machine to work: instructions such as "Add", "Subtract", "Fetch", and so on. But it's hard to see how it could be said to understand anything else.

1.10 Can Searle beat the "Systems Reply"?

Searle discusses some objections to his argument. The most important is what he calls the "Systems Reply". Here is one way of putting it:

> Searle inside the Chinese Room is doing essentially the same tasks as the computer's CP. His argument depends on that assumption, which is perfectly correct. So if operating the rule-books C* fails to provide him with an understanding of Chinese, then running the program C fails to provide the CP with an understanding of Chinese.
>
> But whoever said the CP, taken on its own, could understand Chinese? We never did. The CP is one system, consisting of the

computer's memory, ALU and control unit. But the computer as a whole is a larger system of which the CP is only a part. There are also the input and output units. In addition, we must distinguish between the CP without a program and the CP running a particular program. Whether or not a computer is a serious candidate for intelligence depends on its program: stupid program, stupid behaviour. So it would never make sense to regard the CP on its own as a candidate for intelligence. What *is* a candidate is the system, which is made up of the CP running a suitable program.

Compare a human being. A person with a functioning brain is a system with many parts. Just because the whole system is intelligent, we don't conclude that every part of it must also be intelligent – a single neurone, for example.

It is therefore beside the point that neither Searle nor the computer's CP understands Chinese. The question is whether the whole system – the Chinese Room system as a whole, or the computer running C – understands Chinese. To that question Searle's argument provides no answer.

Searle's opponents generally agree that the Systems Reply is the decisive objection: it is worth taking time over. Notice, however, that it is no *more* than an objection to the Chinese Room argument. If sound, it shows that the argument fails. It doesn't also show that the Chinese Room would genuinely understand Chinese. Showing that an argument for a proposition *p* is unsound doesn't prove that *p* is false!

Searle has a counter to the Systems Reply. It is that he *memorizes* C*, so that the rest of the Chinese Room is "just a part of him"; and he is now the same as the whole system. He seems to think it is embarrassingly obvious that this settles the matter – in addition to which he thinks it plainly absurd that a thing like a room with a man inside it should be capable of intelligent thought. But is he right that by memorizing C* he ensures that he now includes the system as a part?

This is tricky. Suppose that in order to make C* convincing, the programmers made the system express (in Chinese, of course) a strong admiration for the works of Hegel. Searle, however, (we may pretend) dislikes that philosopher's work. So what C* makes Searle say in Chinese (which he himself still doesn't understand) is actually *contradicted* by what he says in English! In that case it would be extremely odd to say that the system was just a part of Searle. At best it would make him strangely inconsistent. In any case this point shows that it is not enough just to *assert* that if he memorizes C*, it is just a part of him.

The argument is not just against behaviourism. At one point Searle seems to suggest that his opponents maintain that provided the system can fool the Chinese, it understands Chinese. In other words, he seems to suggest that they are committed to behaviourism: the view that (roughly) having thoughts and feelings is just a matter of behaviour and behavioural dispositions. (Behaviourism and the idea of dispositions will be discussed in Ch. 5.) No doubt many of his opponents actually are behaviourists. But they are by no means *all* behaviourists. What they are committed to is that it is in theory possible that there should be a program which endowed a computer system with *the ability to understand* a language such as Chinese. They could perfectly well agree that the system's overt behaviour wouldn't settle the matter, and that it makes a crucial difference how the internal processing is done.

Notice, however, that the Chinese Room argument has the resources to take account of this view. Certainly, if the argument works at all it works against behaviourism. But if it works at all it works also even against AI enthusiasts who are *not* behaviourists. The reason is that C is assumed to be any program which actually *does* enable the machine to understand Chinese. If that requires a special kind of internal processing as well as the right patterns of behaviour, C is assumed to provide them. It's just part of the original assumption.

1.11 A further point about computers

At this stage in the discussion in his original paper Searle claims that "The whole point of the original example was to argue that such symbol manipulation by itself couldn't be sufficient for understanding Chinese in any literal sense" (1980: 359f; see also 362). I find this surprising, since that point seems quite different from the main point of the Chinese Room argument. What Searle says in the words just quoted is independent of the Chinese Room argument itself. It is very powerful, and not undermined by the Systems Reply. Imagine that on some remote planet, uninhabited by any living things, or by anything else with intelligence, there were a computer (just a computer, not a robot) running a program like C. It wasn't put there by space-travellers; it wasn't designed by an intelligent being; it came into existence over thousands of years by cosmic fluke. Could we sensibly say that a computer in that situation understood Chinese, or indeed anything at all?

It is extremely hard to see how words could be meaningful if they were deprived of connections with the kinds of things we would suppose they were about. Suppose this computer, sitting by itself on a lifeless planet, were to produce a sequence of marks which a Chinese reader would have translated as meaning "There are rabbits in Wales". Would the fact that it produced that sentence imply that *the sentence meant anything to it, the computer?* How could it be meaningful if (as we are assuming) it has no connection with rabbits, much less with Wales? (See Wittgenstein 1953: *passim*; Putnam 1981: 1–5; and §9.3.)

Having offered his riposte to the Systems Reply, Searle goes on to attack another objection, which he calls the "Robot Reply". In effect the Robot Reply concedes the point just discussed, but says:

> Even if a computer on its own couldn't understand a language, a computer-controlled robot, suitably programmed, could.

Searle's reply is to invite us to put the Chinese Room inside the robot, and to complain, as before, that he still doesn't understand Chinese. I leave it as an exercise for the reader to consider how Searle's opponents ought to respond.

1.12 An important general class of machines

> "Could a machine think?"
> The answer is, obviously, yes. We are precisely such machines.
> (Searle 1980: 368)

That may seem puzzling, coming from Searle. But he points out that his objection is to the claim that a suitably programmed *computer* could think, not to the claim that *some* kinds of machine could think. However, his remark does raise the important question of what to count as a machine from the point of view of the thesis of mechanism. Here is an introduction to a particular class of "abstract machine": a useful formalization of the key features of a very large class of machines.

A simple coffee-vending machine will illustrate the main points. Given it is in good working order, its behaviour can be fully captured in terms of its possible inputs, its possible outputs, and its possible internal states, as I will explain shortly. Assume we can push any of three buttons marked "MILK", "SUGAR" and "CONFIRM", one at a time but in any order. Pressing "CONFIRM" without having pressed "MILK" will ensure no milk; pressing it without having pressed "SUGAR" will ensure no sugar. (Forget about payment: the price is the same for all four types of drink.) Now, the machine's possible inputs are these: "MILK", "SUGAR", "CONFIRM". Its possible outputs are: coffee without milk or sugar; coffee with milk but no sugar; coffee with sugar but no milk; coffee with milk and sugar. But what about its possible *internal* states?

The machine needs a set of different internal states to ensure that it can "take account" of the various possible input combinations. If the customer presses "MILK" we want the machine in effect to "remember" this; similarly if the customer presses "CONFIRM" without having pressed "MILK" we want it to take account of this too; and correspondingly for the "SUGAR" button. *These different internal states amount to a primitive sort of memory.* That is one reason I think it worth spending time over these ideas. Systems with memory may be capable of interesting behaviour.

In fact this machine needs just three possible internal states. (Some people find that surprising.) One is an "initial" state, which we can call "0", which it is in when ready for the next customer, and which it will go into when it has delivered a cup of coffee. It also needs a state M to register that the "MILK" button has been pressed, and a third, S, to register "SUGAR". It does *not* also need a state to register that both "MILK" and "SUGAR" have been pressed, or a special state corresponding exclusively to the input "CONFIRM". What the machine does – in effect its set of "behavioural dispositions" – is fully characterized by the "machine table" opposite.

Input	Current state	Next state	Output
"MILK"	0	M	Pour milk
"SUGAR"	0	S	Add sugar
"CONFIRM"	0	0	Coffee: no milk or sugar
"MILK"	M	M	No action
"SUGAR"	M	0	Coffee with milk and sugar
"CONFIRM"	M	0	Coffee with milk, no sugar
"MILK"	S	0	Coffee with milk and sugar
"SUGAR"	S	S	No action
"CONFIRM"	S	0	Coffee with sugar, no milk

Examples in words: *First line*: when the machine is in its initial state (represented by "0") and the "MILK" button is pressed, it goes into state M and pours milk into the cup. *Fifth line*: when it is in state M and "SUGAR" is pressed, it goes back to its initial state and delivers coffee with milk and sugar. Pressing "CONFIRM" when it is in its initial state will make no difference, as the *third line* of the table shows.

Such a machine is, in the jargon, a *finite deterministic automaton*. It has a finite number of possible states, a finite number of possible inputs, and a finite number of possible outputs. At any given instant it is in one of those states and may be receiving one of those inputs; and when it is in a given state and receives a given input, its next state and its output are thereby determined. Its entire workings can therefore be represented by means of a machine table similar to the one for the coffee machine. There are numerous systems whose behaviour can be accounted for on the basis that they are finite deterministic automata.

A standard computer is of course a prime specimen of a finite deterministic automaton. However, surprisingly, there is no altogether straightforward way to represent its workings on those lines. Part of the trouble is that even for a machine designed to work in certain very well-determined ways, and even on the assumption that it is working properly (which experience suggests is a bit unrealistic), the question of what the inputs, outputs and internal states are depends to some extent on our decisions. Should we treat just any keystroke as a single input, for example? Not every keystroke has an effect on the machine: whether it does depends on what program is currently running. For that reason we might decide to count as inputs only those keystrokes that have effects on its current program. Similar decisions are needed for outputs and internal states. Now, if there is some arbitrariness in deciding what are the inputs, outputs and internal states of a computer, there must be more in trying to fix on them for other systems, and even more for living creatures. For that reason, any attempt to bring human and other living organisms into the framework provided by the idea of a finite automaton will always be to some extent an idealization.

A deterministic automaton with *infinitely* (denumerably) many possible states is the most general sort of *Turing machine*. (Uninitiated readers had better be warned: a Turing machine is *not* a machine capable of passing the Turing Test (see §5.9). The coffee machine discussed above is a Turing machine, as is any computer. But the coffee machine doesn't even look like a candidate for passing the Turing Test, any more than a computer running a stupid program.)

1.13 A shaky assumption

A certain weighty assumption prevailed in the early years of work in AI. This was that the appropriate way to model cognitive processes was in terms of the processing of stored "sentences", analogous to the sentences of a language, which represented beliefs, desires and other intentional states. In the light of that "sentence-processing assumption" it was natural to assume that if a machine were to be capable of producing statements as human beings do, then it would have to be by the operation of the rules of its program on such stored sentences. Understandably Searle seems to have shared the sentence-processing assumption – hence much of the appeal of his Chinese Room argument at the time it was devised.

But the sentence-processing assumption has become increasingly hard to defend over the past few decades. A fundamental consideration is that the workings of a single system can be described and explained at a number of different *levels*. Computers provide especially clear illustrations of this point. One very low level of description and explanation might deal purely in terms of the transmission of sequences of high- and low-voltage impulses along the machine's wires. A slightly higher level would cover transfers of sequences of 0s and 1s from memory to the ALU, from the ALU to various memory locations, and so on; for, as we saw earlier, there is a sense in which these are the only operations the machine performs (§1.7). But we can also describe the machine's operations in more interesting ways. Among a vast number of other things, it might be described as "calculating the paypackets for the employees in a large firm", "working out a diagnosis for a medical condition", or "playing chess". In fact we are forced to use such higher-level descriptions if we want to be able to tell people what we want machines to do, or to describe and explain their workings intelligently and economically.

Those points bear on our conception of cognition generally, and on how we approach a scientific understanding of cognitive processes. If we are glued into the old sentence-processing assumption, we are likely to go wrong in a number of ways. A further powerful consideration has also been undermining the sentence-processing assumption: there is now an alternative way of modelling cognitive processing. It is known as "connectionism" (see §§7.6–7.7).

There is another famous philosophical argument against mechanism. It attempts to exploit Gödel's (first) incompleteness theorem: one of the most remarkable mathematical results of the last century. Presenting and discussing this anti-mechanist argument adequately would be out of place in an introductory book; but a few words may encourage you to pursue it if you are interested.

Gödel's incompleteness theorem shows that (roughly) for any consistent formal system which is sufficiently strong for elementary arithmetic, there is a well-formed sentence of the system which on defensible assumptions any good logician can discover to be true, yet which is not provable in that system. (Under the intended interpretation the sentence is to the effect that it is itself not provable in the system.) The attempt to use this result against mechanism starts from the reasonable assumption that any machine is "a concrete instantiation of a formal system" (Lucas 1961: 44). On that basis, if mechanism is true, every human being instantiates a formal system. It is further assumed that in that case, since many people can do elementary arithmetic, the formal systems they instantiate (if mechanism is true) will correspondingly have to be adequate for elementary arithmetic, in which case Gödel's theorem applies to them. Suppose, then, that some logician Alf is the "concrete instantiation" of a formal system S. By Gödel's theorem there will be a sentence G of S which any competent logician can tell is true, yet is not provable in S. Alf will therefore be able to see that G is true.

However, if he were a machine he could not do so (so the argument goes). The conclusion is that Alf does not after all instantiate a formal system, and mechanism is false.

I believe the only reason this argument once appeared plausible was the sentence-processing assumption. That made it easy to regard stored sentences as the system's axioms, and its program as the system's rules of inference. The sentences produced by the machine as a result of operations performed on its stored sentences could then be regarded as theorems of the formal system it supposedly instantiated. In addition it was reasonable to assume that if the system worked at all, it must be consistent.

All of that made it easy to think that there was something in the appeal to Gödel. However, it is vulnerable at several places (on which see "Further reading" at the end of the chapter). I will note just one, which relates to the above points about different levels of description and explanation. It is clear that if a human organism is to be regarded as instantiating a formal system, it must be at a relatively *low* level of description. How a computer's workings are described at higher levels depends to some extent on interpretation; the same goes for a human organism. It could only be the detailed workings of brain and body that were candidates for characterization in purely mechanical terms. So suppose for argument's sake that those low-level processes can be represented as the workings of a finite deterministic automaton. In that case, of course, it is equivalent to a formal system. But there is no reason whatever to suppose that a formal system representing those workings must *itself* be adequate for elementary arithmetic. "Doing arithmetic" is one of the much higher-level descriptions which apply to the workings of the system as a whole: it does not also have to apply to the churnings of the neurones. That consideration shows that the attempt to use Gödel's theorem against mechanism was mistaken.

1.14 Conclusion

Although Snoopy certainly has no thoughts or feelings, it has guided us towards some main features of the mind–body problem. However, if a more complex type of robot could have thoughts or even feelings, then the construction of such a robot would seem to solve the mind–body problem at a stroke. That provided a motive for examining Searle's Chinese Room argument, one of the two main philosophical arguments against mechanism, which in the end we found unsatisfactory. The second main argument – based on Gödel's theorem – we have only glanced at. However, even if both arguments are defective, it doesn't follow that mechanism is true. Some other objection to it may be decisive – perhaps one or more of the arguments for dualism that will be considered in Chapter 2.

One important conclusion to have emerged is that Searle was right to maintain that a computer on its own (contrasted with a robot) cannot properly be said to understand what it may seem to think or say (see also Chs 5 and 7). Another is that one and the same organism or system may be considered at different levels of description and explanation (see also §5.6). In addition, our examination of arguments against mechanism has raised interesting questions that will be pursued later, notably these: Does it matter what stuff a system is made of (see §6.3)? What determines whether a given system is a genuine subject of thoughts or feelings, rather than just a clever simulacrum (Chs 5, 7 and 8)? Is the system's behaviour all that matters (Ch. 5)? Or does everything depend on its internal "representations" (Ch. 7)?

Main points in Chapter 1

1. The "mind–body problem" has three main divisions: consciousness, intentionality and the relations between physical and psychological explanations (§§1.1, 1.2, 1.4).
2. Science alone does not seem to be enough to solve it (§§1.3, 1.4).
3. Several common objections to the claim that suitably programmed computers or robots could genuinely understand and think are mistaken (§1.8).
4. Searle's Chinese Room thought-experiment is interesting and thought-provoking (§1.9). But his responses to both the "Systems Reply" and the "Robot Reply" fail to do them justice. The Chinese Room argument appears to be defective (§1.10).
5. On the other hand, it is highly plausible that a computer without sense receptors or control of behaviour could not understand anything (§1.11).
6. The coffee-vending machine illustrates an important general

category of machine: the finite deterministic automaton (§1.12).
7. It is important not to presuppose the "sentence-processing" model of information storage and processing, which seems to have misled not only Searle but those who have attempted to use Gödel's theorem against mechanism (§1.13).

Further reading

On the mind–body problem in general Robert Wilkinson (2000) gives careful introductory discussions with detailed texts from Descartes. Gilbert Ryle's *The Concept of Mind* (1949) is a readable, thought-provoking classic. Ryle influenced Daniel Dennett, whose collection *Brainstorms* (1978a) remains very helpful. See also Armstrong (1968); Burwood *et al.* (1998); Chalmers (1996); P. M. Churchland (1988); Dretske (1995); C. McGinn (1982); the last nine essays in Putnam (1975a); Tye (1995); and two collections in particular: Block *et al.* (eds) (1997); Lycan (ed.) (1990). See also the numerous encyclopaedias of philosophy and philosophy of mind that have been produced in recent years and offer useful material on our topics.

Chalmers (1996: 52f., 65–9), gives helpful explanations of possibility and so on, in the context of the mind–body problem.

For his views on essences and related ideas (such as his use of the examples of games and "family likeness") see Wittgenstein (1953), and Kenny (1973: 153, 163). For Quine's, see Quine (1960: 195–200).

For an excellent introduction to the philosophical issues in AI together with more on computers, see Copeland (1993), which includes many useful references. Dennett (1978c) is a valuable discussion, as are other essays in Dennett (1978a).

Searle's Chinese Room argument was originally presented in Searle (1980). It is discussed in many places, including Copeland (1993: 121–37, 225–30), and Dennett (1991: 435–40).

On the crucial idea of levels of description see Hofstadter's instructive dialogue "Prelude . . . Ant Fugue" in Hofstadter & Dennett (1981). The classic attempt to refute mechanism using Gödel's incompleteness theorem is Lucas (1961). It has been attacked in many articles. See for example Dennett (1978a: 256–66) and Kirk (1986).

2 | Is there something extra?

Many people feel that no machine of any kind could have thoughts or feelings because these activities involve something non-physical. Certainly our brains and sensory systems are immensely complex, even more complex than computers. But we can know all that and still suspect that no quantity of nerve cells and fibres, no amount of electro-chemical impulses from neurone to neurone, no flushings around of chemical neurotransmitters and neuroinhibitors, facilitating and blocking signals across however many billions of synapses, could possibly add up to thoughts or feelings. Imagine smelling freshly roasted coffee or feeling rain on your face or hearing the faint cry of a marsh bird in the distance on a still evening. Or think of reading about what the government is planning to do and getting indignant about it; or wondering whether to go to France this summer; or gradually coming to realize that the person sitting opposite finds you attractive. How could such thoughts and feelings be just a matter of physical processes?

2.1 Dualism

If you think there is something extra, beyond the merely physical, then you are some kind of *dualist* (unless of course you think there is not even anything physical anyway, in which case you are an *idealist*). Why should anyone be a dualist? One consideration is that thoughts, emotions, feelings, sensations and conscious experiences generally just *seem* utterly different from physical things. Another consideration is that at least one form of dualism provides for the possibility that the soul survives death. In addition, some people believe in extra-sensory perception, or even in ghosts – phenomena which, if real, are inconsistent with the laws of physical nature as we know them.

Our remote ancestors must have been struck by the fact that a living person breathes and a corpse doesn't. It was easy to think of the breath as something that had departed, leaving the "inanimate" body lying there, cold and motionless. That encourages the belief that this special "breath of life" itself survives death. Hence one possible origin for beliefs about the soul. However, "folk" beliefs are rough and ready: there are more sophisticated versions of dualism. The most influential was put forward by the French mathematician and philosopher René Descartes in the seventeenth century. According to Descartes human beings are a compound of two very different kinds of thing. There is the body, which is solid, and whose characteristic feature is that it is extended in space. There is also the mind (or soul). The characteristic feature of the mind is that it thinks. Not only is it fundamentally different from the body, it can exist without it – which nicely provides for the possibility of survival. Yet Descartes recognized that mental activity affects our behaviour, hence the world; and that the world affects our sense organs, hence our assessment of our situation, hence our decision-making, hence our minds. He thus recognized that there is a two-way cause-and-effect relationship between mind and world. That makes his position a variety of "interactionist" dualism. Are there any compelling arguments for it?

2.2 Descartes's metaphysical arguments for dualism

According to Descartes's kind of dualism – "Cartesian dualism" – the mind is one thing, the body another. He called them two different *substances*, maintaining that each could exist without the other. He had two very different types of argument for his view.

The first arises from his project of doubting everything that could be doubted, with a view to discovering something indubitable: a foundation stone for certain knowledge. His first conclusion was the famous "cogito": I think therefore I am (*cogito ergo sum*). He concluded that *he could not possibly doubt that he existed*; so he knew he existed. But doubting is a type of thinking; so he also knew that whatever else he might be, he was "a thing that thinks": "that is to say, a thing that doubts, perceives, affirms, denies, wills, does not will, that imagines also, and which feels" (1968: 107). He couldn't consistently doubt that he was a thinking thing because doubting itself is a variety of thinking: the very act of doubting that claim was sufficient to prove it true. On the other hand, he reasoned, he *could* consistently doubt the evidence of his senses, for he knew they sometimes deceived him. Pursuing the project of universal doubt, he found he could even doubt whether he had a body. He was able to perform this particular feat by reflecting, as we noted earlier, that there might just possibly be a malicious demon controlling his experiences. This demon would give him all the experiences he would have had if he had really been in his study, walking about, sitting in his chair at his table, and so on – while really there were no such things: no physical world at all. The whole history of the experiences he had ever had from his senses – apparently the experiences of a person perceiving a world populated by human and other bodies – would in that case be like a particularly consistent and long-lasting dream. (I leave it to you to decide whether this thought-experiment is harmless, or just an "intuition pump".)

Wrenching ourselves away from Descartes's reflections on the possibility of *knowledge*, which is not our topic, let's note a crucial step in his argument for the distinctness of his mind (or soul or spirit) and his body. It is that he thought he was consistently able to suppose that his *body* didn't exist. He concluded that he himself – this thinking thing – was not physical. Descartes offered more than one version of this argument: I will concentrate on the one in the Sixth Meditation. A crucial step is the assumption that if it's possible for me to "conceive clearly and distinctly one thing without another", then, since "all the things I conceive clearly and distinctly can be produced by God precisely as I conceive them", I can be "certain that the one is distinct or different from the other, because they can be placed in existence separately, at least by the omnipotence of God" (1968: 156). Here is a brief summary of this version of Descartes's reasoning (not in his own words):

(D1) I cannot consistently doubt that I exist.
(D2) I cannot consistently doubt that I am a thinking thing.

(D3) I can consistently doubt that my body exists.
(D4) If I can "conceive clearly and distinctly one thing without another", then I am "certain that the one is distinct or different from the other".
(D5) Therefore my body is not the same thing as myself.
(D6) Therefore I am a non-physical thinking thing.

Now, if premises (D1), (D2), (D3) and (D4) are all true, it seems that (D5) must also be true, from which, given (D2), (D6) must be true as well. If that is right, this version of Descartes's argument is at least valid. If in addition those premises are actually true, then the argument is also sound, in which case we must accept the conclusion. (D1) and (D2) are hard to dispute for the reasons Descartes gives. (D3) is also accepted by many philosophers. What about (D4)?

Here is what looks like a counter-example to (D4): the heavenly body we know as the Evening Star. It's one thing to know that this planet (Venus, in fact) is the Evening Star, and something else – something that it takes difficult measurements and comparisons to establish – to know it's *the same one* as the Morning Star. So it seems I can "clearly and distinctly" conceive of the Evening Star without conceiving of it as the Morning Star. If that is right, then by premise (D4) of Descartes's argument, I ought to be certain that the Evening Star is "distinct or different from" the Morning Star, and could exist without it. But because I know it isn't different, I'm not certain of any such thing.

Is that really a counter-example? It's possible to doubt that it is. Even when we know the Evening Star is the Morning Star, we also know it would still have been the Evening Star if it had been equally prominent in the evening sky, but some other planet had been prominent in the morning sky. However, that doesn't help Descartes. Consider what he is trying to do. He is trying to show that (a) the mind is a different *thing* from the body; (b) the mind can exist without the body. It is not enough for his purposes to show that just *being a mind* is different from being a body. We can accept that it is; but that doesn't mean minds can exist without bodies. Even though, in a sense, being the Evening Star is different from being the Morning Star, the Evening Star and the Morning Star are one and the same thing. Given they are the same thing, the Evening

Star cannot exist without the Morning Star. That counter-example remains a problem for this argument. However, the type of reasoning Descartes uses in his argument continues to be influential, as we shall see later (§4.7).

2.3 Descartes's empirically based arguments for dualism

In addition to his metaphysical arguments, Descartes appeals to empirical considerations. He thinks matter alone is incapable of performing the functions performed by minds. To make this point vivid he invites us to consider animals. He thinks animals are purely physical organisms whose behaviour can be understood as the result of mechanical processes. They are automata; human beings are not.

Suppose there were machines which looked and behaved like human beings "inasmuch as this were morally possible". Two things would unmask such machines. One is that they could not use language as we do. It is a remarkable fact that we are able to produce and understand any of an infinite number of sentences; or rather, since memories and lives are limited, we can produce and understand an *indefinitely* large number of different sentences. Animals lack such creative abilities, according to Descartes.

The second thing that would unmask a human-like automaton is its inability to produce appropriate behaviour in all sorts of different situations. We have *reason*; animals and machines don't. Again, Descartes concedes that animals and machines can to some extent behave in apparently rational ways; but insists it is mere appearance and occurs:

> simply through the disposition of their organs: for, whereas reason is a universal instrument which can serve on any kind of occasion, these organs need a particular disposition for each particular action; whence it is morally impossible to have enough different organs in a machine to make it act in all the occurrences of life in the same way as our reason makes us act.
> (1968: 156)

There were no computers in the seventeenth century. Descartes seems to have assumed the only way for a machine to produce a given pattern of behaviour was for that precise pattern to have been anticipated by its constructors and a special mechanism devised to produce it in response to a particular stimulus. It would be what psychologists and neurologists call a "reflex". Descartes's objection is thus the same as Objection 2 in §1.8; but he has the excuse that computers had not been invented in his day. He could hardly have foreseen that computer programming would make it possible for machines to produce responses that had not been "hard-wired" but resulted from the workings of the machine's program.

2.4 Causation: desperate theories

Cartesian dualism provoked a tremendous amount of discussion. The problem his contemporaries found most pressing was this: if mind and body are so fundamentally different, how can they interact?

Recall that he claimed mind and body were radically different kinds of thing. The essence of mind is to think; the essence of body is to be extended in space. The mind is not extended in space; the body is. The mind is indivisible and has no parts; the body is divisible and has parts. His contemporaries and later philosophers had particular difficulty in conceiving how two such different sorts of thing could have effects on one another.

Various alternative theories were suggested. One was *occasionalism*. According to this theory, only God really causes things to happen. The mind doesn't cause the body to move, nor does the body affect the mind. Instead, what seem to us like causes are merely the "occasions" for God to bring about what we think of as their effects. My deciding to go and get a cup of coffee is the occasion for God to make my limbs take me to the kitchen. My tooth decaying is the occasion for him to make me feel toothache. (Malebranche was a principal exponent of this way out.)

Another alternative theory, proposed by Leibniz, applied not just to minds and bodies but to all cases of (what we call) causation: *pre-established harmony*. He used the example of two clocks in perfect agreement. Suppose one indicates twelve and the other strikes twelve. It might seem that the first event caused the second; but in fact they occur as they do because they are preset to work in parallel. Similarly, Leibniz suggested, the mental and physical lives of the universe have been preset by God to run in parallel.

Those alternatives to Cartesian "interactionist" dualism are pretty desperate attempts to overcome the problem of mental–physical causation, and I will not spend more time on them. In any case you might wonder whether the problem is that serious. Certainly it is a problem if you assume that all cases of causation necessarily require a picturable mechanism. But why should they? There are indeed plenty of causes and effects that turn out to be comprehensible in terms of mechanisms whose workings we understand. (What caused that bridge to collapse? The river had been gradually wearing away the foundations. What causes the moving pictures on the screen? Light is projected through a succession of images on a film.) But when it comes to the fundamental facts, such as (perhaps) the natural laws of electromagnetism, there seems no room for mechanisms that we can comprehend. We just have to accept that things behave in accordance with these laws, and there is no more to say. Perhaps, then, if there is mental–physical causation on the lines Descartes claimed, we have to accept it as a basic fact about the world. (He himself made a similar point in correspondence with Elisabeth of Bohemia.)

Other opponents of Descartes rejected dualism altogether. One alternative position was materialism, defended vigorously and intelligently by Thomas Hobbes, among others. Another, put forward by Spinoza, was that the world has two "aspects". On this account God and nature are one and the same. As for the mind–body problem, Spinoza's view was that the mental and the physical are also two aspects of the same thing. In itself this thing is neither mental nor corporeal; but it presents itself in two different ways.

That "dual-aspect" idea is attractive. If it is right there can be no serious problem of mind–body interaction: mind and body are not two different entities, just the same entity under different aspects. However, merely asserting that there are two aspects doesn't take us very far. One problem is the nature of the single entity which supposedly has these two aspects. A more pressing problem is to understand what it is for there to *be* two aspects. What does it take for the mysterious underlying something to present itself under its "mental" aspect, and what does it take for it to present itself under its "corporeal" aspect? Those questions are so hard that the dual-aspect theory has few supporters – even if we ignore what Spinoza said about God and the universe and concentrate on the mind–body problem. (There is a significant possible exception: Thomas Nagel, some of whose ideas will be considered in Ch. 4.)

2.5 Trouble for Cartesian dualism

Although a great deal is still not known about the workings of the brain, a great deal is known. It's known that the brain consists of a vast number of different types of nerve cells or *neurones* – up to one hundred billion of them; with an even vaster number of interconnections – up to ten thousand for a single neurone. It's known that electrochemical impulses travel along nerve fibres from cell to cell; that each cell is capable of "firing"; and that whether or not a given cell fires on a given occasion depends on how it is connected to other cells, and on whether the transmission of an impulse is facilitated or blocked by the chemicals known as neurotransmitters and neuro-inhibitors. It's known further that our ability to retain and recall information depends on our brains working properly; that damage to certain areas of the brain results in impairment of certain sorts of ability connected not only with memory, but with a whole range of cognitive abilities, including those concerned in perception, thought, planning and use of language. Alzheimer's disease, for example, causes damage to brain cells and to their delicate interconnections, and this is what causes its sufferers to lose their memories, their abilities to plan, and their intellectual powers generally.

The more is discovered about the workings of the brain, the less room there seems to be for any contribution from a Cartesian mind: it seems redundant. If a good memory and intellectual powers generally depend on a properly functioning brain, and interference with the functioning of the brain impairs memory and other intellectual powers, then a non-physical mind has little if anything to contribute. How can *it* be what does the thinking, when every day brings additional scientific evidence that the capacities we exercise in thinking depend on the brain? To put the same point differently: if the mind is what thinks, how can it get on without a brain? What could it possibly do without memory, for example? It is tempting to conclude that the mind just *is* the brain – which is one version of "physicalism", to be examined in Chapter 3.

Those considerations help to explain why physicalism is attractive, and why the Cartesian form of dualism is hardly taken seriously by scientists and philosophers today, except to illustrate how not to solve the mind–body problem.

Those points are reinforced when we reflect on the causation of events in the brain. Neuroscientists routinely assume that events in the brain are caused by other physical events. Indeed, they share with other scientists the general assumption known as the causal "closure" or "completeness" of the physical domain:

All physical events are caused by other physical events.

It is true that today's physics tells us events at the micro-level are probabilistic, not deterministic. But that doesn't seem to provide a loophole for *non*-physical events to be involved. (At most it requires us to rephrase the assumption on the lines of: to the extent that physical events are causally explicable at all, they are explicable in terms of other physical events. For our purposes we can safely ignore this complication.)

All the evidence fits the assumption that all physical events are caused by other physical events. (See Papineau 2002 for an account of how this has come to be established.) But if Cartesian dualism were true, there ought to be vast numbers of brain events *not* caused by other physical events but, instead, by the workings of the Cartesian mind. If a Cartesian mind causes brain events, then they are not caused by other brain events; such causal gaps ought to be detectable by brain scientists. It follows that the more evidence we continue to accumulate that there are no such gaps, the stronger the case against Cartesian dualism. And since we are talking about *interactionist* dualism, there ought to be gaps in the other direction too: brain events which fail to cause other brain events because what they cause are non-physical events in the Cartesian mind. There is no more evidence of that sort of gap than of the other sort.

2.6 Property dualism

Since the scientific evidence is running so strongly against Cartesian dualism, those who still think there are reasons to reject physicalism tend to adopt, instead, a dualism of *properties*. Descartes himself said the mind is a "substance", by which he meant it was capable of existing by itself, or at least without the body. The body is a substance too, being obviously capable of existing without a mind – if only when dead. Property dualists accept there is no such "substantial" mind. They also accept that we have bodies and brains with all sorts of physical properties, such as *weighing 86 kg*, and *being composed of a bony skeleton, muscles, nerves, heart, blood vessels, brain, skin*. Brains have such properties as *being composed of an enormous number of neurones and nerve fibres*, and *being almost split into two hemispheres*. But property dualists say we also have distinctively mental properties, which are non-physical. Just what these special non-physical mental properties are is not universally agreed, but they include some involved in intentionality and some involved in consciousness. Under the first heading there might be *thinking about Paris; wanting a cup of coffee; believing there are tigers in India*. Under the second heading there might be *feeling pain; experiencing the blue of the sky; having a greenish-yellow after-image*.

If Cartesian dualism has to be given up, powerful considerations seem to push us towards property dualism. On the one hand it is hard to suppose that the mental properties just mentioned are not *real*: it is hard to be an "eliminativist" about them (see §3.9). Yet if they are real they are hard to accommodate in the purely physical world; and if they really can't be accommodated in it they must be non-physical. Now, one notable fact about the physical world is that it is subject to certain universal, highly general *laws*. These laws seem to have no place for either thinking or feeling: either for intentional properties or the qualitative properties apparently involved in the phenomena of consciousness. Suppose I am thinking about Paris. How could whatever enables my thought to hit that particular city be brought under the laws of physics? This, however, is something on which a great deal of philosophical work has been done in recent years, and it continues to be a vigorously debated area of the philosophy of mind. We shall examine some current views later, especially in Chapters 5 and 7. Meanwhile it is at any rate possible to see why reflection on the phenomena of intentionality should nudge people towards dualism.

Reflection can also suggest that the phenomena of *consciousness* are, if anything, even more difficult to fit into the purely physical world than the phenomena of intentionality. It's true that we seem capable of grasping explanations of sensations such as pain purely in terms of neurophysiology. We can see how pain receptors are activated by damage to the skin; how impulses from them are transmitted to the brain; how the patterns of neural activity thus produced are processed in other areas of the brain. Yet understanding that sort of thing seems on the face of it quite consistent with the total absence of sensations; indeed, it can still seem so even after much reflection. It *seems* intelligible that all those processes should be capable of occurring without there being "anything it was like": without the individual concerned being "phenomenally" conscious (see §§4.6–4.11 on "zombies").

If that is right (*if* it is), then the special properties needed to account for consciousness are non-physical. However, property dualism needs a lot of clarification. One thing we urgently need to know is: what is meant by saying the special properties are "non-physical"?

2.7 A test for commitment to dualism

A neat test for whether you are committed to dualism is owed to a metaphor (or thought-experiment) of Saul Kripke's (1972). He invites us to imagine God creating the physical world: suppose God fixes the distribution of all the elementary particles with all the details of their states and positions across the whole of space-time. Now, having fixed the entire *physical* universe, does God have to do "something in addition" in order to ensure that human beings have thoughts and feelings? If you reply "No: by fixing the purely physical universe God *thereby* fixes the mental or psychological facts, including all the facts about our thoughts, feelings, emotions and conscious experiences", you are a physicalist. If on the other hand you insist that fixing the purely physical facts about the world is not enough to fix the mental or psychological facts, you are some kind of dualist. (Actually you might also be an idealist. Instead of saying everything is physical, or that there is a mix of physical and non-physical, idealists say that everything is mental. I will ignore this option. By the way, it should be clear that Kripke's thought-experiment is harmless. The test, stripped of metaphor, is simply whether or not you claim that the purely physical facts are alone sufficient to fix the psychological facts.)

Let us apply this test to property dualism. Imagine God's blueprint for the universe was strictly in terms of an idealized version of today's physics, which for our present purposes we can assume is true, and that this specification was as close as possible to the actual universe but introduced no bits of non-physical vocabulary. Now imagine God creates the universe (past, present and future) in accordance with that specification. Since the specification fits the actual universe as far as possible, and since (surely we agree) that means it covers at least all *inanimate* parts of the universe, God will thereby have created the things we call "mountains", "valleys", "rivers", "plains", "rolling country" and whatever other items we describe in our unscientific talk about the landscape. Yet by definition those ordinary landscape descriptions are not included in the specification because they are not part of the austere vocabulary of physics. It's just that we know the purely physical specification guarantees that those landscape descriptions *also* apply to things in the universe so specified. It follows that the purely physical specification guarantees that the earth's surface has these properties among others: *has mountains*; *has valleys*; *has rivers.*

Are those properties to be counted as physical or as non-physical? Ordinarily we would surely say they were physical. Yet they were not specified in terms of physics. Indeed, it is plausible to say they are not even *definable* in terms of physics. (One reason is that it seems there could have been landscapes in universes which had different physics from our own.) If that is right, physical properties had better not be said to be definable in purely physical terms. That would result in classifying as non-physical some properties that were by any ordinary standards physical.

Talking in terms of mountains, valleys, rivers and the rest is thus *a different way of talking* about exactly the same realities as are also describable in terms of the austere vocabulary of physics. The austerely physical descriptions classify things and events according to one scheme, a scheme arrived at as a result of quite recent, highly disciplined, informed, critical attempts to discover the ultimate nature of the physical universe, and requiring much detailed use of scientific instrumentation. The landscape vocabulary in contrast classifies things according to a scheme arrived at as a result of a long history of mainly unsophisticated people aiming to characterize their surroundings in ways that they and others could easily understand and use. The imaginative exercise with God creating the universe makes clear how it is that the landscape vocabulary applies to the same physical universe as the austere physical one.

We noticed just now that if you think that having created the universe according to his purely physical specification, God had *no further work to do* in order to create thinking, feeling creatures, then you are a physicalist; while if you think he *did* have further work to do, you are a dualist. This Kripkean test for commitment to dualism is not always acknowledged for what it is. As we shall see when we examine some early versions of physicalism in the next chapter, many philosophers used to assume that so long as the problematic properties were asserted to be "identical" with physical properties, then there would be no problem for physicalists even if God would have had to do further work in order to provide for such identities; and there are plenty of philosophers who continue to take that line.

Just calling the special mental properties "non-physical", then, is not enough to make clear whether or not you are a property dualist. If you intend to imply a commitment to dualism, you must accept that the presence of those properties is not guaranteed by the creation of a universe specifiable in austerely physical terms. In that case you must concede there is a possible universe which is an exact duplicate of ours in all respects describable in austerely physical terms, but without those properties. If on the other hand you think the existence of the properties in question *is* guaranteed by the creation of a universe specifiable in austerely physical terms, then you are not a dualist after all, and it is misleading to describe yourself in that way. From now on, therefore, I will take it that "property dualism" describes only those conceptions according to which the special mental properties are *not* guaranteed to exist solely by the existence of a universe that fits a specification in austerely physical terms (see also §3.11).

2.8 Trouble for property dualism

Once those points have been digested it becomes clear that property dualism faces serious difficulties. If the special mental properties are non-physical by definition, and therefore not provided for by the purely physical facts, how do they fit in with those facts?

The most natural reply is that there are *causal* relations between physical properties and non-physical mental ones. But again we have to take account of what is known. As we have seen, scientists have good reason to accept the causal closure of the physical (see §2.5). It is at least highly probable – many would say it is known – that all physical items in the brain are caused by other physical items. (I use "item" to apply to things, events and properties.) Whatever physical item may be present in the brain, scientists look for a physical explanation. True, we don't yet know absolutely everything about the workings of the brain, so there is theoretically some small space for non-physical causes to play a role. But each day scientific research strengthens the evidence for the view that there are no such causes. If that is right, any non-physical mental properties there might be are causally idle. That conflicts with the natural assumption, which we saw Descartes shared, that mental events such as experiences of pain, or decisions and intentions, are causal factors in the production of physical events.

It remains possible that although the supposed non-physical properties don't themselves cause anything physical, they may be caused *by* physical items. But if property dualists are forced to adopt that position, very few other philosophers today are willing to follow them. It is *epiphenomenalism*, to be discussed below. Even fewer, if any, are willing to go further and claim there is no causation in either direction: either from the mental to the physical, or from the physical to the mental. That is *parallelism*.

2.9 Epiphenomenalism

The points just emphasized about the physical explicability of physical items in the brain (and elsewhere) were accepted by some scientists and philosophers as long ago as the nineteenth century. These thinkers were impressed equally by the overwhelming power and comprehensiveness of physical explanations and by the apparent impossibility of explaining all mental properties as physical. According to epiphenomenalism, human beings are complex physical systems, and all physical processes in them are explicable physically; however, some of these physical processes cause non-physical mental phenomena. The physical world is still supposed to be "closed" under causation: every physical event is still supposed to be physically caused. For that reason those non-physical mental phenomena, though caused by physical events, themselves have no physical effects. They are mere "epiphenomena".

Epiphenomenalists know that their position conflicts violently with ordinary untheoretical beliefs. We ordinarily believe that our mental states affect what we think and do, especially what we say. We take it that those events, including our conscious experiences, produce whatever physical movements are involved for example in speaking and writing about those very mental states, *including our conscious experiences*. It seems pretty well incredible that those conscious experiences should none the less have no effects on the physical world. All the same, epiphenomenalists are persuaded that their considered reasons for their position outweigh mere shock-horror reactions. They accept the completeness of physics: they agree with their opponents that there is no room for non-physical events to have effects on the physical world. But they challenge their opponents to account for the facts of (especially) phenomenal consciousness without having to appeal to non-physical items.

A consideration which seems damaging to epiphenomenalism is that we seem able to *talk about* such things as phenomenally conscious mental states. According to a very widespread view about aboutness (or intentionality), it depends on causal relations between words and the things those words refer to, or are about. For example, it is widely held that I can think about and refer to Paris only because my use of the name "Paris" has an appropriate causal relation with that city. (There are exceptions: we can think and talk about extraterrestrials without having interacted causally with them. But they seem explicable in terms of indirect causal relations – we understand "terrestrial" first by virtue of our causal relations to the earth; hence can grasp the notion of beings from outside it.) If conscious experiences have no causal role in bringing about our utterance of expressions like "conscious experiences", it is hard to see how those expressions can refer to the conscious experiences themselves. How can they refer to *them,* rather than to the physical processes which, according to epiphenomenalism, cause them?

Evolution poses another difficulty for epiphenomenalism. Since evolution cannot select for what has no effects on the physical world, it is hard to see how evolutionary pressures can have had any effect on whether or not consciousness evolved. Nor is it any use pleading that consciousness, like the weight of the polar-bear's fur coat, may be just a necessary by-product of those purely physical features that *have* been selected for. Why should it have occurred at all, if we could have got on perfectly well without it? Even more to the point, why should creatures have evolved that spend a vast amount of time apparently *talking* about their conscious experiences, when according to epiphenomenalism, equally intelligent and efficient creatures *without* conscious experiences could have evolved too – and would have had the evolutionary advantage of saving a lot of time and energy?

2.10 The "Cartesian Theatre"

Gilbert Ryle in his classic *The Concept of Mind* ridiculed Cartesian dualism as the "myth of the ghost in the machine". His target was the model of the mind or soul – rather like the audience in a theatre – witnessing a parade of mental phenomena. His objection to this picture was that it just pushes the original problem a stage further back. The original problem was to understand what it is to have thoughts, emotions, desires and so on. The proposed solution – the model of the "Cartesian Theatre" – invites us to understand it on the model of an internal viewer witnessing thoughts, emotions, desires and so on as if on a private television screen. But that tells us nothing about the internal viewer and nothing about the nature of this "witnessing", except that it is like perception. If the internal witnessing really is like perception, and if perception generally has to be explained on the Cartesian Theatre model, then in order to explain it there has to be a further-back internal viewer, with a further-back witnessing of a parade of thoughts, emotions and so on – and we are launched on an infinite regress. It is vicious, since it has nothing to tell us about the nature of perception except that it is like perception. If, however, the internal witnessing is not much like ordinary perception, then the model of the Cartesian Theatre fails to explain what it *is* like, and we are still in the dark.

Thanks to that infinite regress objection of Ryle's, the Cartesian Theatre model of mental activity is widely rejected. At any rate it is rejected when clearly recognized. However, quite often it seems to exert a hidden influence on our thinking about the mind. Nor is this influence restricted to the ways dualists picture the mind's workings. It continues to affect the reasoning of philosophers and scientists who profess to be hard-nosed physicalists (see Dennett 1991: 101–39 and *passim*). When you read any account of the nature of the mind, especially one purporting to explain consciousness, it's a good idea to ask yourself whether it is covertly influenced by the Cartesian Theatre model.

2.11 Conclusion

Although both intentionality and consciousness are extremely hard to account for if they are purely physical, the arguments for dualism are less than compelling – and its difficulties are formidable. Here is a further consideration. Even though we may find it hard to understand how a purely physical system could have thoughts and feelings, how does it help to say that something *non*-physical must be involved? Just being non-physical is obviously not enough by itself to explain thinking or feeling. Why shouldn't there be unconscious, unthinking non-physical things? Dualism just takes for granted that there is something special about non-physical minds or properties that accounts for consciousness and intentionality in a way not open to further comprehension. That makes it no better than the ghost of a solution to the mind–body problem. Let us see whether physicalism offers a way out.

Main points in Chapter 2

1. Descartes's metaphysical arguments for dualism, though interesting, are fundamentally flawed (§2.2).
2. His empirical arguments, too, don't stand up to developments in science and technology (§2.3).
3. The doctrines of occasionalism and pre-established harmony are desperate expedients to avoid problems with mind–body causation (§2.4).
4. There is overwhelming evidence that events in the body are caused by other physical events, which entails that the Cartesian mind is redundant (§2.5).
5. Kripke's image of God creating the universe provides a useful test for commitment to dualism (§2.7).
6. Property dualism faces a similar problem to Cartesian dualism:

there seems no room for non-physical properties to have physical effects (§2.8).

7. But epiphenomenalism is not just counter-intuitive (as its exponents know); it faces further severe difficulties (§2.9).

8. The Cartesian Theatre model of mental activity seems worse than useless, yet continues covertly to influence thinking about the mind (§2.10).

Further reading

On Descartes (1596–1660) above all read his *Meditations*. His *Discourse* is also readable and interesting. Kenny 1968 is a useful introduction. References in the text are to the Penguin *Discourse on Method and the Meditations*. The standard English translation of his works is Cottingham *et al.* Descartes (1984–91).

On Leibniz's (1646–1716) doctrine of pre-established harmony see G. H. R. Parkinson's collection: Leibniz (1973).

Kripke (1972) uses his image of God creating the world towards the end of Lecture III.

Thomas Nagel (1986) anticipates a possible dual-aspect approach. It is hard to find unambiguous support for property dualism. Davidson (1970) is a classic text often cited, but by no means clearly in favour of it. Chalmers (1996) defends a version of property dualism and epiphenomenalism.

On the Cartesian Theatre see Ryle (1949) and Dennett (1991).

On idealism see Foster (1982).

3 Physicalism

We noticed that the assumption of the closure of the physical – that all physical events are caused physically – is reinforced with every bit of brain research. This assumption rules out Cartesian dualism because it rules out the thought that non-physical events are involved in causing events in the brain or anywhere else. The only varieties of dualism for which it might seem to leave room are epiphenomenalism and parallelism; and we have already noted some difficulties with those positions. Empirical facts about the brain and central nervous system, and about how bodily events are caused, thus provide a powerful motive for adopting some variety of "materialism" or "physicalism". In this chapter we will examine a range of physicalist approaches to the mind.

3.1 What is physicalism?

Philosophy has always been concerned with the question, "How do we fit into the rest of the world?" Obviously we have a lot in common with apes, some things in common with cats and dogs, less with insects, even less with flowers and trees. As for stones, rivers, clouds, planets and other inanimate things, we appear to share only the fact that we are more or less solid and take up space and time. But as early as the fifth century BC certain Greek thinkers devised the first version of the atomic theory.

The Greeks were (rightly) perplexed by the phenomena of change such as combustion, digestion and decay. How could sticks become fire, smoke and ashes? How could the athlete's porridge vanish and muscle appear? Surely nothing can come into existence from nothing, and nothing can disappear altogether. Such reflections eventually resulted in the idea that everything is made up of atoms and empty space. There are infinitely many of these atoms (the word means "uncuttables"). They come in different shapes and sizes. Some are rounded and smooth, some hooked, some sharply pointed. Many are too small to be seen. The different properties of things are explained in terms of the different shapes, sizes and arrangements of their atoms. Water flows because its atoms are smooth and rounded; rock is solid because the shapes of its atoms lock firmly into one another and cannot easily be split apart. Human beings too are nothing but complex structures made up of atoms. This ancient theory was put forward in conscious opposition to other theorists who (some two thousand years before Descartes) maintained that the soul is completely different from the ordinary physical furniture of the world, and sharply distinguishes human beings, or at any rate animate creatures, from other things. The atomists held that having a "soul", or being "intelligent", is explained by the presence in living bodies of certain very small, very smooth spherical atoms, which move rapidly about the body and cause our limbs to move. When we die these atoms just trickle out through the gaps in our bodies: there is no persisting immortal soul.

This ancient form of atomism is a prime example of "materialism", arrived at by philosophical and (proto)scientific reasoning. It is a *metaphysical* theory because it claims to tell us about the fundamental nature of what there is. According to it, nothing exists but atoms and empty space.

You get a different materialistic position if you base it on modern physics. There are various ways of doing this. One is to say that what exists fundamentally is whatever modern physics tells us there is. So whatever exists is made up of the items said to exist by particle physics or string theory or whatever, together with whatever that implies. One thing that seems to many philosophers to count powerfully in favour of this version of materialism is that modern physics is so strikingly successful.

The ancient atomic theory seemed like a good account of what people came to think of as "matter": something extended in space and more or less solid or resistant to pressure. Modern physics teaches there is actually nothing like the Greeks' atoms – *nothing* is solid and impenetrable. So the name "materialism" has come to strike some philosophers as misleading; they use "physicalism", and I will follow them.

There are varieties of physicalism. Some physicalists are concerned only to explain how the facts of mental life can be reconciled with the apparent fact that we live in a purely physical world. They just want to make it *intelligible* how it is that there are thoughts and feelings in a physical universe. This project is sometimes referred to as "naturalism". (A recent book by Fred Dretske is called *Naturalizing the Mind* – his aim being to show how puzzling aspects of mentality, such as consciousness, can be understood in such a way that they can be seen to fit unproblematically into the rest of the natural world.) Others have a more ambitious agenda. An extreme aim, originally proposed by the scientists and philosophers of the Vienna circle in the 1920s and 1930s, was to establish the "unity of science". Carl Hempel summed up this doctrine as follows: "all the branches of science are in principle of one and the same nature; they are branches of the unitary science, physics" (1935: 382). It is a variety of "reductionist" physicalism (the notion of reduction will be examined later in §3.8).

The *evidence* for physicalism in general is nicely summarized by Quine's remark: "Nothing happens in the world, not the flutter of an eyelid, not the flicker of a thought, without some redistribution of microphysical states" (1981: 98). But that will not serve as a *statement* of physicalism because it is consistent with dualism. Dualists who accept the causal closure of the physical have to concede that the laws of nature ensure that nothing happens without something physical happening. But they can still insist that nature is not wholly physical, and that some physical events are always paralleled by non-physical ones. In this way they can apparently continue to maintain a restricted variety of dualism in the teeth of the evidence that *physical* nature is governed by laws that take account only of physical things and events. (Apparently: we shall notice serious problems with this sort of dualism towards the end of Ch. 4.) So what are the options for physicalists? One is behaviourism; but it will be convenient to put off discussing behaviourism until Chapter 5. Perhaps the most natural form of physicalism is the "identity thesis".

3.2 The psycho-physical identity thesis

The idea is simple. In J. J. C. Smart's words, "Sensations are nothing over and above brain processes" (1959: 56). Neuroscience offers suggestions about what brain processes are going on when we experience pain, for example, and the identity theorist asserts that pain just *is* the occurrence of those processes. Suppose the relevant process in the case of pain is the firing of C-fibres. (It is known that this particular example is too simple but it is standard.) Following that suggestion the psycho-physical identity thesis tells us:

(P1) Pain is identical with C-fibre firing.

One objection is that pains have properties that brain processes don't have. Pains may be stabbing, or burning, or throbbing, for example; but it makes no sense to say brain processes have those properties. The point is particularly obvious for the case of visual sensations such as after-images. Suppose you are experiencing a yellowy-green after-image. According to the identity thesis that after-image is identical with some process in your brain. But brain tissue is greyish or pinkish, and brain processes don't have colours such as yellowy-green.

A good reply to that "property objection" is that it isn't the pain or the after-image that is being said to be identical with the brain process, but the *having* of the pain or the after-image. So we get such revised claims as:

(P2) Having a pain is identical with having one's C-fibres firing.

The property objection loses its grip on that version of the identity thesis, since no one can say that having a pain (or, equivalently, being in pain) is throbbing or stabbing. The theorist can just say that it is having a stabbing pain that is identical to having one's C-fibres firing (in some particular way), and that it is having a greenish after-image that is identical with some other brain process.

Two further difficulties with the psycho-physical identity thesis cannot be disposed of so quickly. The first was raised by Saul Kripke.

3.3 Kripke on the necessity of psycho-physical identities

The identity thesis was standardly put forward as *contingent*. It seemed obviously a question of empirical fact whether the neural process supposedly identical with the person's having pain was the firing of C-fibres or something else. How could pain *necessarily* be identical with that particular kind of brain process? However, Kripke advocates an approach to reference and naming according to which certain expressions pick out their referents by necessity. By that he means they refer to the same thing in every possible world. He argues that this is true especially of proper names. The name "Aristotle", for example, applies to that same individual person in every possible world – regardless of what the contingent facts about that person might be in that world. In the actual world that individual was a great philosopher, who for a time tutored Alexander the Great. Conceivably, though, there is a possible world where that same person – the individual referred to by the name "Aristotle" – never meets Alexander the Great and never even becomes a philosopher. His being that particular individual does not in Kripke's view depend on his taking up any particular occupation.

Expressions which in that way have the same referent in every possible world (at least, in every world in which they refer at all) are called "rigid designators". Kripke argued that many expressions other than proper names are also rigid designators, and he included among them both words for psychological states, such as "pain", and scientific terms designating processes in the brain, such as "C-fibre firing". On that basis he concluded that the psycho-physical identity thesis ought to be regarded as *necessary*, not merely contingent. For if both "pain" and "C-fibre firing" are rigid designators, applying to exactly the same things in every possible world, then if it is true in the actual world that pain is identical to C-fibre firing, there is *no* possible world where that same statement is not true. In other words it is true in every possible world, which means it is necessary. ("Hold on!" you may object; "The meanings of the words may be different in different worlds, in which case the statement is not true in every possible world." But that objection is off target, since when we assert the identities we are using our *own* actual-world language, with its own meanings.)

Perhaps it doesn't seem too much of a revision of the psycho-physical identity thesis to reclassify it as necessary rather than contingent. So what? Here Kripke has a further point to make. He thinks it is obvious that such identity statements *cannot* be necessary. For example he thinks it is obvious that there could have been C-fibre firing without pain. He also thinks it is obvious that, conversely, there could have been pain without C-fibre firing. Rather on the lines of Descartes's argument for the distinctness of mind and body, Kripke argues that the essence of pain is to have a certain feeling, not to have a certain physical make-up.

To summarize Kripke's reasoning: if the psycho-physical identity statements in question are true, then, because "pain" and "C-fibre firing" (for example) refer to the same things in every possible world, those statements are necessary. But the statements cannot be necessary because we can easily conceive of the mental states in question being present without their associated physical processes. Therefore those identity statements are not necessary. Therefore, given the earlier conclusion, they are not true either – and physicalism is false.

There was and continues to be controversy over Kripke's reasoning; not only over his overall views on rigid designators but also over his claim that "pain" is a rigid designator, and (especially) over his claims about what is possible. I will leave the introductory discussion of Kripke's ideas there.

3.4 Worries about type-identity

Now let us take a look at the other main difficulty that seems to face the psycho-physical identity thesis. The first thing to notice is that the thesis as stated purports to be true of whole *types* of mental states (as contrasted with individual instances: *tokens*). For example, thesis (P2) in §3.3 purports to tell us about *all* pains, not just the pains of human beings, and certainly not just those of one individual, or of one individual at just one time. It is a thesis of *type-identity*. As you brood over that point the thesis starts to appear too strong to be credible. Suppose it is true that C-fibre firing is what goes on when human beings are in pain. Can we be sure the same is true for cats and dogs too? After all, their brains are in several ways unlike ours. Even if it is true for cats and dogs, can we be sure it is also true for all kinds of creatures that we suppose capable of suffering pain? What about extraterrestrials? Is the only possible way to be capable of feeling pain to have nervous systems like ours?

How can we justify such a strong assumption? Nor is pain the only sensation to be taken into account. If the identity thesis is to be any use for the purpose of making it intelligible that what exists is purely physical, it must apply to *all* kinds of sensations and experiences. (Many identity theorists do indeed take the thesis to apply to all kinds of mental states, including the "intentional" ones.) Instead of some reasonably neat neural process being the one supposedly identical with having pain, it starts to look as if there is an indefinitely large number of candidates.

Nor is that the only way to press this difficulty for the type-identity thesis. We can approach the matter from the point of view of neuroscientists researching the mechanisms of pain. What makes them so sure it is the mechanisms of *pain* they are dealing with, rather than, say, the mechanisms of tickling? It's not as if they started their investigations already knowing that C-fibres are involved (assuming they are involved at all). At some stage they knew no such thing. All they knew was that human beings do feel pain; they wanted to discover which neural processes underlie it. Now, what led them to think it was pain and not tickling was that they knew the types of behaviour typically associated with pain: winces, groans or screams, depending on the degree of damage to the bodily tissues involved; dispositions to take pain-killers; and so on. So when they started their investigations they had no idea whether they would discover just one single type of neural activity associated with pain. Conceivably they might have discovered, to their surprise, that human beings fell into two or more different classes. The pain mechanism for one of these classes might involve C-fibres; for another it might involve X-fibres. One thing the scientists would *not* conclude, if that surprising result turned up, is that only one lot of human beings really felt pain and the rest didn't. Instead they would conclude that there are two or more different mechanisms for pain. All of which encourages the same conclusion as before: in principle if not in fact, the same type of sensation could be underlain by different physical processes: it is capable of being "realized" in any of a number of different ways. That is the so-called "multiple realizability" objection to the type-identity thesis. It is widely regarded as a powerful consideration.

Physicalists impressed by the multiple realizability objection have tended to respond in either or both of two main ways. One is to substitute a weaker thesis: one of "token"-identity, to be discussed shortly (p. 58). The other is functionalism, which must wait until Chapter 6. First, though, let us take another look at what can seem like a problem for physicalists: mental causation.

3.5 Physicalism and mental causation

We saw that according to epiphenomenalism – a dualistic thesis – mental states and events are caused by, but do not themselves cause, physical ones. Since we normally suppose that our thoughts and feelings are among the main influences on our behaviour, and so make a real difference to our lives and the world, that doctrine is hard to accept. It seems ridiculous to say my headache had nothing to do with my taking an aspirin, or that your deciding to open this book had no effect on your actually opening it. For such reasons, most psychologists and philosophers reject epiphenomenalism and accept some variety of physicalism. But that seemingly reasonable choice has uncomfortable consequences of its own.

Physicalism includes the closure assumption: all physical events are caused by other physical events. But in that case how does the *mental* come into the story? How can there be room for causal explanations in mental terms? Interactionist dualists have no problem here, of course, since according to them many physical events can only be explained by reference to mental ones. On their account mental events are non-physical, but still play a vital role in the causal order. Physicalists in contrast have to see mental events as just a special kind of physical events. And then it can seem mysterious that mental explanations should have any role to play. Does mind matter?

That question arises in an interesting way when we consider Donald Davidson's "anomalous monism". First, though, we had better consider some general points about psychological explanation.

3.6 Psychological explanation

Suppose I slam the door. In the circumstances that behaviour might be explained by my being angry. Slamming doors is typical of angry people, although of course different people express anger in different ways (a more controlled person might have just pursed their lips). Or suppose you are uncertain about the meaning of "anomalous" and open a dictionary. The natural explanation of that action would be in terms of your wanting to check the meaning of that word, and believing you could get the necessary information from the dictionary. We are constantly describing and explaining our own and others' behaviour in similar terms. Emotions such as anger, love, hate, fear, anxiety, elation, are one group of states we appeal to in our everyday psychological explanations. Alongside emotional states and feelings we appeal to beliefs, desires and other "intentional states" (sometimes called "propositional attitudes") such as intentions, wishes, hopes, or suspicions. Unless our thinking has been influenced by philosophy we tend to assume that (a) there really are such emotional states as well as states of believing, wanting, intending and the rest; and (b) these states interact causally to produce behaviour. Assumptions (a) and (b) are characteristic of everyday or "folk" psychology. (The term "folk psychology" is used to emphasize comparisons with "folk medicine" and other unscientific systems of belief.) But both (a) and (b) are subject to vigorous philosophical challenge, as we shall see. A third important point is that many, perhaps most, folk-psychological explanations have the following characteristic pattern (when what is to be explained is why a subject *s* who wants something *w* performs an action *a*).

1. All things considered, *s* wants *w*;
2. *s* believes that doing *a* will, in the circumstances, give *s* the best chance of getting *w*;
3. *s* does *a*.

(When we are offering such explanations in everyday life we don't always fill in all the details. If we are driving and you suddenly jam on the brakes, you might simply say, "I thought that little girl was going to run into the road" – you wouldn't need to add: "and (i) I wanted to avoid hitting her; (ii) I believed that putting on the brakes would help to avoid hitting her".) There is also vigorous philosophical debate on the extent to which this pattern applies, and how it relates to other types of explanation, notably to explanations in the physical sciences. We shall take note of the most significant of the contending views in the course of the book, starting with Davidson, who insists on a strong contrast here.

3.7 "Anomalous monism"

Davidson is impressed by the differences between everyday psychological explanations and the sorts of explanations we find in natural science. Scientific explanations rest on deterministic laws that purport to be "strict": they apply quite generally, without qualification. Everywhere and any time, for example, the heat in a closed system flows from hot regions to cold ones. But there seem to be no such strict deterministic laws for psychology: none governing mental events alone; none governing relations among mental and physical events. Although my slamming the door might be explained by my being angry, we could hardly claim there was a *strict law* on the lines of "Whenever Kirk is angry he slams the door". The whole basis on which we describe and explain behaviour in terms of thoughts and feelings seems very different from the basis on which we describe and explain the workings of systems in terms of physics. Many philosophers hold that in order to produce a satisfactory belief–desire explanation we have to take account of the *whole* system of the subject's intentional states at the time, not just of one belief or one desire. Davidson agrees. He maintains that the physical and mental schemes of explanation have "disparate commitments". Physical explanations appeal to strict laws. Psychological explanations "are responsible to the background of reasons, beliefs, and intentions of the individual" (1970: 222):

> We know too much about thought and behaviour to trust exact and universal statements linking them. Beliefs and desires issue in behaviour only as modified and mediated by further beliefs and desires, attitudes and attendings, without limit.
>
> (1970: 217)

Davidson also maintains that if one event causes another event, there must be a law covering that relation. And he maintains, like virtually everyone except epiphenomenalists and parallelists, that there actually *are* causal relations between mental events and physical events. So we have the following three theses:

(M1) "At least some mental events interact causally with physical events."

(M2) "Events related as cause and effect fall under strict deterministic laws. (. . . the Principle of the Nomological Character of
Causality)."

(M3) "There are no strict deterministic laws on the basis of which
mental events can be predicted and explained . . . (The
Anomalism of the Mental)."

(Quotations from Davidson 1970: 208)

At first sight (M1)–(M3) appear inconsistent. If (M1) mental events
cause physical events, then by (M2) both physical *and* mental events
must be covered by strict laws. But (M3) rules out strict psycho-
physical laws. There is, however, a way out, Davidson claims: to
recognize that one and the same event may be both physical and
mental. Each individual mental event is *identical* with a physical one.

How does Davidson reconcile the "nomological character of
causation" with the "anomalism [or 'lawlessness'] of the mental"?
The key is that whereas "causality and identity are relations between
individual events no matter how described", "laws are linguistic", so
that whether or not a given event instantiates a law depends on how
that event is described. A given individual event may be described as
my thinking about Paris, and under *that* description it doesn't figure
in any strict laws on Davidson's account. But the same event may
also be described in purely physical terms; and when it is it can
perfectly well figure in the statement of some strict law. So my
thinking about Paris can cause some piece of behaviour, such as the
movements of my hand as I pick up a book, even though no law
covers those events *under those descriptions.*

That will serve to illustrate Davidson's argument for the identity
of mental events with physical events. We know (he assumes) that
mental events such as my thinking about Paris cause physical events
such as hand movements. So the principle of the nomological
character of causation entitles us to infer that there are descriptions
under which the two events instantiate a strict law. By the anomalism of the mental that strict law cannot be in psychological terms.
The only alternative is that it is in physical terms, from which it
follows that the events in question have physical descriptions. In
other words they are physical events (Davidson 1970: 224).

"Anomalous monism", then, is the position just illustrated. It
claims that all events are physical. But it is not committed to the

identity of mental *types* with physical types; only to the identity of every individual mental event – every "token" event – with a physical event. In this way anomalous monism avoids the problems raised by multiple realizability: the plausible view that any given type of mental event is capable of being realized in an indefinitely large number of different ways. You will also probably have noticed that anomalous monism rules out the view that each type of mental state is *definable* in physical terms. For if mental state types were definable in purely physical terms, then at least some laws covering mental–physical interactions in purely physical terms would be equivalent to laws where, by using such definitions, physical terms were replaced by psychological terms. There couldn't be such laws if Davidson is right about the "lawlessness" of the mental.

One interesting objection to anomalous monism is that, in Jaegwon Kim's words, it seems to entail that "mentality does no causal work". Kim assumes that mental properties could be somehow sliced off from the physical properties they actually accompany, and connected up with others. He says:

> the very same network of causal relations would obtain in Davidson's world if you were to redistribute mental properties over its events any way you like; you would not disturb a single causal relation if you randomly and arbitrarily reassigned mental properties to events, or even removed mentality entirely from the world. (1989: 269).

For, he asserts, "on anomalous monism, events are causes or effects only as they instantiate physical laws, and this means that an event's mental properties make no causal difference".

However, Kim's reasoning depends on a heavy assumption: that it is *possible* that things should have retained their actual physical properties even if they had had different mental properties. If that is a genuine possibility his objection has great force. But what if the physical properties fix the mental ones because they actually *constitute* or *realize* them – because *it takes no more for there to be those particular mental properties than for there to be those physical ones?* We shall examine that idea in more detail in the following sections. For the moment it is enough to note that if physical properties *do* constitute mental ones, then the mental properties are not causally idle at all. Being constituted by physical properties, they cause whichever events are caused by those physical properties. Kim would probably reply that although Davidson maintains a thesis of the "supervenience" of the mental on the physical, his version of it is too weak to block the objection. We will examine the notions involved in that thesis shortly. First it will be useful to consider the more general idea of reduction.

3.8 Reduction

The ancient atomists held that all that exists is atoms and empty space. Evidently people objected that lots of other things existed too, for example colours and tastes. The atomists replied that "By convention there is colour, by convention there is sweetness, by convention there is bitterness; but in truth there are atoms and empty space" (the words are those of Democritus, one of the originators of atomism). In that way human beings and their thoughts and feelings are elegantly included in the rest of the universe. They involve nothing special – apart, perhaps, from their specially complex structure. In *one* sense of the word "reduction", then, the ancient atomists "reduced" everything to atoms and empty space. In that same sense later materialists such as Hobbes reduced everything to forms of matter; and contemporary physicalists reduce everything to whatever physics tells us are the ultimate constituents of the physical universe.

Reduction in that sense just marks physicalism off from dualism, so there is no interest in arguing that physicalists are committed to it: of course they are. There are, however, other senses of "reduction" in which it is not at all clear that physicalists are compelled to be reductionists.

The reductionist's central thought, as it applies to the reduction of one theory to another, is roughly this:

All the explanatory and predictive work of the reduced theory can be done by means of the reducing theory.

The most straightforward way to reduce one theory to another would be to show that the expressions of the first have translations or at least logical equivalents in terms of the second. (I take it two statements are logically equivalent if a contradiction follows from saying one is true while the other is false.) A suggestion that this could be done for the special case of the reduction of psychology to physics emerged from the work of the Vienna Circle. Hempel proposed that all psychological statements are translatable into statements of physics:

> All psychological statements which are meaningful, that is to say, which are in principle verifiable, are translatable into propositions which do not involve psychological concepts, but only the concepts of physics. The propositions of psychology are consequently physicalistic propositions. Psychology is an integral part of physics. (1935: 378)

However, if psychological states are multiply realizable it is hard to see how they could possibly be translated into physical terms, even in a wide sense which lets in mere logical equivalents. To cover all the different ways in which a given mental state M could be realized, the physical-language translation would have to specify each of them. At best it would be a very large disjunction, on the lines of:

> "x is in mental state M" is equivalent to "x is in physical state P1 or P2 or . . . or . . .".

If there were only a finite number of ways in which M could be realized, then no doubt it would be possible to claim that such equivalences held. But if there are indefinitely many different ways in which M could be realized, no such physical statement is available: it could not be spelt out. And quite likely there are indefinitely many such ways. For the equivalence would not only have to cover the different ways in which terrestrial creatures are constructed, it would have to deal with all the creatures in the universe capable of being in mental state M. Further, there can be no reason why the only possible way for psychological states to be realized is by precisely the types of physical entities and laws that actually exist. Not even the most enthusiastic members of the Vienna Circle suggested that we know a priori that the *actual* physics of the universe is the only one there could have been. For that reason alone it seems impossible for there to be a disjunction of the kind that would be required to cover all the ways of being in mental state M.

A number of weaker varieties of reduction have therefore been suggested. One kind resorts to "bridge laws" which link the theory to be reduced to the reducing theory. The following biconditional might serve for the special case of pain:

(B) x is in pain if and only if x's C-fibres are firing.

Note that it would not be enough for (B) just to *happen* to be true: it must hold by natural or "nomological" necessity. Now, (B) contains predicates from both psychology and neurophysiology. So, as you may have noticed, this proposal is vulnerable to the multiple realizability objection just as much as the one which envisaged equivalences. It is also vulnerable to the decisive objection that in any case, from the point of view of our interest in explaining *physicalism*, nomological correlations would never have been enough. For epiphenomenalist and parallelist dualists could consistently concede that mental events and physical events are connected by natural law.

There are other ways of conceiving of reduction than the ones mentioned above; but they are the most familiar. (For recent alternative approaches see P. S. Churchland 1986; Bickle 1998.)

3.9 Eliminativism

In §3.8 we noted Hempel's claim that psychology is translatable in terms of physics, and is indeed "an integral part of physics". Some philosophers are even more radical. They are sceptical about psychology itself, or at least about folk psychology, and suggest it will eventually be replaced by the developed neurosciences. When that time comes, they think, we shall see that it was little more than a sham, and that there are really no such things as the mental states it purports to describe and explain. That is *eliminativism*.

The most vigorous recent exponent of eliminativism has been Paul Churchland. He says:

> Eliminative materialism is the thesis that our commonsense conception of psychological phenomena constitutes a radically

false theory, a theory so fundamentally defective that both the principles and the ontology of that theory will eventually be displaced, rather than smoothly reduced, by completed neuro-science.   (P. M. Churchland 1981: 206)

He argues first that "folk psychology" really is a theory rather than, for example, a set of more or less disjointed beliefs, or (as some hold) a craft, a body of know-how or a collection of techniques.

Each of us understands others, as well as we do, because we share a tacit command of an integrated body of lore concerning the law-like relations holding among external circumstances, internal states, and overt behaviour.   (1981: 207)

He points out that other "folk theories", such as folk medicine, have been superseded long since, and goes on to emphasize what he sees as the three main shortcomings of this "systematic, corrigible, speculative theory" (1981: 210).

First, folk psychology (FP) "sheds negligible light" on numerous cases of "central and important mental phenomena" such as "the nature and dynamics of mental illness, the faculty of creative imagination, or the ground of intelligence differences between individuals"; or sleep; or our impressive abilities to coordinate eye and hand in catching moving balls; or memory; or the nature of the learning process.

Secondly, the history of FP "is one of retreat, infertility, and deca-dence": both its content and its success:

have not advanced sensibly in two or three thousand years. The FP of the Greeks is essentially the FP we use today . . . In short, FP is a stagnant or degenerating research program, and has been for millennia.   (1981: 211).

Thirdly, when we consider the scientific study of human beings we find an extremely powerful, wide-ranging account of our "constitution, development, and behavioural capacities which encompasses particle physics, atomic and molecular theory, organic chemistry, evolutionary theory, biology, physiology, and materialis-tic neuroscience". This account is:

deliberately and self-consciously coherent with the rest of our developing world picture. In short, the greatest theoretical synthesis in the history of the human race is currently in our hands, and parts of it already provide searching descriptions and explanations of human sensory input, neural activity, and motor control. But FP is no part of this growing synthesis. Its intentional categories stand magnificently alone, without visible prospect of reduction to that larger corpus.   (1981: 212)

In summary he claims:

that FP suffers explanatory failures on an epic scale, that it has been stagnant for at least twenty-five centuries, and that its categories appear (so far) to be incommensurable with or orthogonal to the categories of the background physical science whose long-term claim to explain human behaviour seems undeniable. Any theory that meets this description must be allowed a serious candidate for outright elimination.

(1981: 212)

In spite of the force of this denunciation, relatively few philosophers seem to have taken up eliminativism. Each of his three main points is open to criticism.

First, supporters of FP can concede that it says nothing about vasts areas of huge scientific interest; but point out that it is just a "folk" theory, not a scientific one. It cannot reasonably be expected to provide explanations of *all* the phenomena associated with human mental capacities. Compare *geometrical optics*. It deals well with several noticeable and important properties of light, such as the paths it takes when reflected and refracted in transparent media; but it has nothing to say about such phenomena as polarization, interference and diffraction, or about electromagnetic radiation in general. Geometrical optics offers only partial coverage of related phenomena, but is not for that reason objectionable.

The same example serves to undermine the objection that FP has hardly changed over centuries. Neither has geometrical optics – and the reason is that it is broadly *true* of the phenomena it *does* deal with. Why shouldn't the same hold for FP?

Churchland's third point is perhaps the most important. Supporters of FP may well have to concede that it is highly unlikely ever to be reduced to a completed neuroscience. But why should that be a reason to regard it as *false*? It would be such a reason only if the irreducibility of one theory to another entailed that they could not possibly both be true: only if irreducibility entailed incompatibility. But I know of no good reason to suppose that is so, and some reasons to suppose it is false. To appreciate one such reason it will be useful to consider the notion of *supervenience*, and then that of *strict implication*.

3.10 Supervenience

Although Davidson denies there are psycho-physical laws, he does hold that the mental "supervenes" on the physical. Of course, since he thinks all events involved in causation – in effect, all events – are physical, he could hardly fail to accept some kind of dependence. The special idea of supervenience is roughly that there can be no mental difference without a physical difference. But that is rather too rough for our purposes. What we want is a notion that makes explicit how physicalists do or can – or perhaps should – conceive of the relation between the mental and the physical. Making supervenience suitably clear for this purpose has not proved easy. Kim has usefully clarified some different versions. One of these is *strong supervenience*, which can be defined as follows (for the special case where mental properties are supposed to supervene on physical ones):

(S)   Necessarily, if something x has a mental property M, then there is a physical property F such that x has F and necessarily anything with F also has M.

This means that if Anna has a headache, necessarily there is some physical property F which, if anything has F, it has a headache too. However, while there are physicalists who would agree that (S) is true, they ought to reject it as a basis for physicalism because some dualists could also consistently accept it – at least if the necessity invoked in the last clause is just a matter of natural law. This is because (S) would be satisfied even if mental states were irreducibly non-physical, yet there were laws of nature by which each mental

property was *correlated* with a physical property. Even epiphenomenalists and parallelists could agree with that.

Clearly, then, if supervenience is to do the job of explaining the
commitments of physicalism, the necessity invoked at this point
must be absolute: there must be no possibility at all that the physical
property in question should fail to involve the mental property.

Now let us consider the first occurrence of "necessarily" in (S): is
this kind of necessity absolute or just nomological? If it is absolute,
then any possible occurrence of a mental property must depend on
a physical property. In that case Cartesian dualism is ruled out by
absolute necessity. There have been philosophers who would
accept that view (Hobbes, for example), but no one seems to have
thought up a convincing argument to prove it. As we shall see, it is
possible to be a physicalist without maintaining that there are no
possible dualistic worlds: without maintaining that dualism is necessarily false. In the absence of a good reason to hold that the initial
necessity is absolute, presumably it has to be understood as nomological.

With the first occurrence of "necessarily" understood nomologically and the second understood absolutely, (S) seems to offer
an acceptable statement of the core of physicalism. I will now
describe a rather different way of stating it.

3.11 Strict implication, and a formulation of minimal physicalism

Recall Kripke's image of the creation of the physical universe, which
we can think of in terms of God creating it according to a blueprint
or specification P. To get some idea of what P might be like, pretend
we have an idealized version of today's physics (instead of the
complex of competing theories we have in fact). P can then be a
conjunction of all true statements expressible in terms of that
austere theory. Now, by the Kripke test for physicalism (§2.7)
physicalists must accept that having created a universe in accordance
with P, God would have had no further work to do in order to
ensure that the creatures in that universe had whatever mental states
they actually do have. In creating that purely physical universe he
created the mental universe as well – or so physicalists must hold. In
other words, they must hold that all mental descriptions true in the

actual world apply to things and properties in the purely physical world specified by P.

To put the point another way: physicalists must hold that whatever statements other than those in P may also be true, they are *made true by* whatever is specified by P. They are bound to accept that claim because they hold that nothing exists apart from what is described by P – or rather, nothing exists apart from what is *either* described by P *or* is provided for by what is described by P, in the sense that once the purely physical universe specified by P exists, nothing else is required to make all those other statements true. Mountains and rivers, though not explicitly provided for by P, are provided for by P. To put it in yet another way, which many find particularly helpful: physicalists must hold that all those true non-physical statements are *alternative ways of talking about* exactly the world specified by P. If someone claimed to be a physicalist yet suggested that the true non-physical statements described something additional to what is specified by P, they would in effect be committing themselves to a kind of dualism.

The minimal commitments of physicalism may therefore be formulated in terms of the following *strict implication thesis*. P is defined as before: it is a conjunction of all truths expressible in terms of the austere vocabulary of an idealized version of today's physics. Q is a conjunction of all other truths – apart from (SI.1) and (SI.3) below:

(SI.1) P strictly implies Q.

This strict implication thesis is to be taken to mean that it is absolutely impossible for P to be true and Q false, or that there is no possible world where P is true and Q false.

I hope the paragraph before last makes clear that physicalists are committed to (SI.1) whether they like it or not. I also hope it makes clear what guarantees that the necessity involved is absolute. It is that any physicalist holds that the world specified by P is what *makes true* the other truths, so that these other truths are alternative ways of talking about the world provided for by P. However, (SI.1) by itself is not enough for a statement of the commitments of even a minimal physicalism. One reason is that (SI.1) is logically consistent with its converse: that Q strictly implies P. It seems unlikely that anyone would actually wish to maintain that the non-physically expressible truths should strictly imply all the truths expressible in austerely physical terms; but that needs to be made explicit, both for completeness and in order to help to spell out the idea that the physical fixes the mental, not the other way round. So physicalists are committed not only to (SI.1) but to:

(SI.2)   Q does not strictly imply P.

Even (SI.1) and (SI.2) together are not quite enough. They could both hold in a universe where, in addition to whatever was provided for by P, there were some non-physical thinkers or feelers (angels, perhaps?). To rule that out we need one more thesis:

(SI.3)   There are no true statements other than (SI.1), (SI.2) and those strictly implied by P.

I think (SI.1), (SI.2) and (SI.3) are individually necessary and jointly sufficient for (minimal) physicalism.

I do not maintain that (SI.1)–(SI.3) do more than make reasonably clear what physicalism commits you to. It is particularly important that they do nothing to make clear how on earth it can be that P strictly implies all the mental truths. Indeed, I would say that the philosophical task of making that clear is the main thing still needed for solving the mind–body problem.

One or two further points should be noted. One is that you may be wondering how (SI.3) can be true for logical and mathematical truths; but there is no difficulty here. Either such truths are necessary or they are not. If they are necessary, then it is impossible for P to be true while they are false: obviously *all* necessary truths are strictly implied by P. If they are not necessary, then a consistent physicalist had better hold that they are made true by the purely physical facts – so again there is no problem.

What about laws of nature? Presumably they can be stated in some language or other. If they can be stated in the language of our austere ideal physics, then they already belong to P. If not, then physicalists must hold that they are made true by whatever *is* specified by P, and they are strictly implied by P.

We have noticed that causation is a source of difficulties in connection with the mind–body problem (§3.5). The problem it poses for physicalism is this. If causal explanations in physical terms are true, how do causal explanations in mental terms fit into the story? They threaten to be redundant or false. Theses (SI.1)–(SI.3) offer a coherent way of dealing with mental causation. They are consistent with the following general approach. First, the minimal physicalist notes that P includes not only particular truths about the distribution and states of elementary particles (or strings, or whatever) throughout the whole of space and time; it also includes statements of all physical laws. Given the assumption that the physical domain is closed under causation, P therefore includes the materials for explaining all causal transactions whatever. Now, either there are *also* true causal statements in mental terms – truths not included in P – or there are not. If not, there is no problem for that reason (although we need an explanation of why that should be so). If, on the other hand, there *are* true causal statements in mental terms, then according to (SI.1) they are among the many non-physically stated truths strictly implied by P. They are *made true* by the physical facts provided for by P; in fact they are alternative ways of describing *exactly the same events* that are provided for by P. It follows that if and when we give true causal explanations in psychological terms, they raise no special problems precisely because they explain events that also have descriptions and explanations in purely physical terms.

On that account, true causal explanations in psychological terms cannot be inconsistent with explanations in physical terms. They may, however, be *more explanatory* than explanations in low-level purely physical terms. This is because they use concepts that are more suitable than purely physical concepts for picking out and describing the relevant structures and relationships. (Among other things, psychological descriptions ignore irrelevant microphysical details. For discussion see Putnam 1975c: 295–8; Kirk 1996.) In this way the strict implication thesis offers a satisfying treatment of what have been supposed to be serious problems for physicalism (see for example Kim 1993).

One more puzzle: is (SI.1) itself necessary or contingent? P and Q each include many contingent truths; on the other hand (SI.1) looks as if it should be necessary. A simple example will help to clarify the position. Our garden is infested with rabbits. Suppose I were to say:

(A)   The number of rabbits in our garden at this moment is greater than 5.

Is (A) necessary or contingent? Well, it tells us something about the number of rabbits in the garden, so surely it is contingent. On the other hand, the description "the number of rabbits in the garden at this moment" refers to some definite number. Suppose for argument's sake that number is 10. It is certainly not contingent, but necessary, that 10 is greater than 5. The strict implication thesis (SI.1) has a rather similar structure to (A). In effect (SI.1) says that *the actual world is one where the conjunction of true physical statements, whatever it may be, strictly implies the conjunction of other true statements, whatever* it *may be.* Since that purports to tell us about how things are in the actual world it is contingent – in spite of the fact that it is not contingent whether the first conjunction strictly implies the second. (A key consideration is that "P" refers to the *actual* physical truths, not to whatever the physical truths might happen to be in some non-actual possible world.)

It will be convenient to associate a certain kind of supervenience with theses (SI1)–(SI3). If and only if the facts described by Q stand in the relation specified by (SI1)–(SI3) to the facts described by P, I will say that the Q-facts *supervene logically* on the P-facts. ("Logically" works here exactly as in "logically possible": the Q-facts supervene logically just in case it is logically impossible for the P-facts to hold while the Q-facts fail to hold. For a closely related notion of logical supervenience see Chalmers 1996.)

3.12 Must physicalists be either eliminativists or reductionists?

Physicalists are committed to reductionism in a trivial sense because they maintain *there is nothing else in the world* but what is provided for by physics (see §3.8). Are they also committed to a more interesting variety of reductionism? Kim has argued that they are – or rather, he has argued that they are committed either to reductionism or to eliminativism (Kim 1989). It would take us too far out of our way to examine his reasons in detail. But it is worth remarking that he does not consider what appears to be a way out for physicalists. This is to acknowledge the minimal physicalism represented by theses (SI.1)–(SI.3). If you endorse this minimal physicalism you can easily maintain that there are plenty of everyday psychological truths, in spite of their irreducibility to the narrowly physical truths of P. All you have to do is say that these truths are strictly implied by P.

Churchland simply assumes that materalists, if they regard a given theory as true, are bound to be reductionists about it. (And he is evidently thinking of reduction in some non-trivial sense.) Since he maintains that folk psychology cannot be reduced to the physical in any of the usual senses of "reduction" explained above, he concludes that physicalists must be eliminativists. Kim, on the other hand, thinks physicalists who reject eliminativism must be reductionists (again, in some non-trivial sense). In fact, however, there seems no reason why physicalists who endorse (SI.1)–(SI.3) should be non-trivial reductionists.

If the physical universe is as specified by P, then obviously vast numbers of truths not included in P also hold. To use the example of landscape descriptions from Chapter 2: it is impossible that P should hold and that descriptions such as "mountains", "valleys", "rivers", "plains", "rolling country" and so on should fail to hold as well. By definition those landscape descriptions are not part of the austere vocabulary of physics. Yet we know for certain that the truth of P guarantees that those descriptions *also* apply to things in the universe specified by P. But how do we know it for certain? Is it because we have already somehow reduced the landscape *vocabulary* to the austere vocabulary of physics? Clearly not. It is because we know enough about what matters from the point of view of the application of landscape descriptions to know that they involve nothing over and above the sorts of things that are provided for by P. For example, we know that the existence of mountains involves nothing beyond relatively large-scale arrangements of rocks and other naturally produced materials so that the surfaces of these arrangements project a sufficient distance from their surrounding regions.

This example shows that in general we don't need to know that definitions or other kinds of reductions are available in order to know that cases of strict implication hold. If we do know that strict implication holds, then there is no need to go to the trouble of trying to find detailed reductions of landscape descriptions to narrowly physical ones. If we apply that lesson to the psycho-physical case, it seems we might be able to tell that the strict implication thesis holds without having to find reductions for each individual psychological description. (See Kirk 1996 and 2001.)

Notice that theses (SI.1)–(SI.3) provide not only for all the objects that there are in the universe, but for all their properties too. The Kripke test for physicalism and dualism has in effect been rephrased in terms of these theses. If you think (SI.1)–(SI.3) hold, then you are a physicalist; if not, not. So if in particular you think that all truths about the properties of things are strictly implied by P, then even if you also think that ascriptions of some properties are not reducible to narrowly physical terms, you are not a property dualist but a non-reductive physicalist.

3.13 Conclusion

In this chapter we have examined the main varieties of physicalism and some criticisms of some of them. Although the earlier versions favoured statements of identity, whether type-identity or token-identity, contingent or necessary, it is now quite common to concentrate on some form of supervenience or strict implication. We have also noticed that if the physicalists' aim is just to explain how there can be thinking and feeling in a purely physical world, there is no need for them to be reductionists in any non-trivial sense. However, all kinds of physicalism, not just strongly reductionist versions, face formidable difficulties. We shall examine a few of the most urgent in Chapter 4.

Main points in Chapter 3

1. The main evidence for physicalism is its success in explaining physical events. But merely stating the evidence does not amount to a statement of physicalism: it is compatible with some forms of dualism (§3.1).

2. The psycho-physical identity thesis comes in different versions, each with its own problems. For example, Kripke argued that the identities in question must be *necessary*, and that we can see they are not (§§3.2, 3.3).

3. "Multiple realizability" is another problem for the identity thesis (§3.4).

4. If all physical events are explicable in purely physical terms, how does mentality come into the story? Some have claimed that Davidson's "anomalous monism" is exposed to this difficulty (§§3.5, 3.7).

5. In everyday psychological explanations we appeal chiefly to emotions and "intentional states". We assume these states (a) are real and (b) interact causally to produce behaviour. The explanations also typically have a certain characteristic pattern.

6. There are varieties of reductionism. They do not have to go so far as *eliminativism* (§§3.8, 3.9).

7. The ideas of supervenience and strict implication are useful for constructing statements of physicalism. A formulation of minimal physicalism is offered, and it is suggested that minimal physicalists need not be reductionists in any non-trivial sense (§§3.10, 3.11, 3.12).

Further reading

For physicalism in general see Armstrong (1968), Chalmers (1996, 1999), P. M. Churchland (1988) and Lewis (1994).

For the type-identity thesis see Armstrong (1968), Hill (1991), Kripke (1972), Lewis (1966, 1972) and Smart (1959). For further introductory discussion see P. M. Churchland (1988: 26–35).

On multiple realizability see Fodor (1974) and Putnam (1975c, 1975d).

For more on psychological explanation see §§ 9.1–9.4 and Burwood *et al.* (1998), P. M. Churchland (1988), P. S. Churchland (1986), Clark (1989), Davidson (1963, 1974), Dennett (1987), Fodor (1968), Greenwood (ed.) (1991), M. McGinn (1997), Putnam (1985d), Stich (1983) and Wittgenstein (1953).

For mental causation and anomalous monism see Davidson (1963, 1970), Heil & Mele (eds) (1993) and Kim (1993).

For further discussion of the contrast between psychological concepts and explanations and physical ones see also §4.2; §§9.1–9.4; and McDowell (1985, 1994).

Bickle (1998) surveys and discusses more recent versions of reductionism at length. See also P. S. Churchland (1986), Lewis (1994) and E. Nagel (1961).

For eliminativism see P. M. Churchland (1981) and P. S.

Churchland (1986). There are essays for and against in Greenwood (ed.) (1991).

Kim (1993) contains a number of his papers on supervenience and related topics. See also Chalmers (1996) (who, as well as explaining "logical" supervenience, gives reasons why physicalists are committed to it) and Kirk (1996, 2001).

Some objections to
4 physicalism

Thomas Nagel's paper "What Is It Like to Be a Bat?" (1974) shone an uncomfortably bright spotlight on physicalism. Physicalists had failed to engage with the really difficult question: how to explain consciousness. "Without consciousness the mind–body problem would be much less interesting", he wrote. "With consciousness it seems hopeless." He suggested that for an organism to have conscious mental states is for there to be *something it is like* to be it. There is something it is like for me as I look at the bricks in the wall; there is nothing it is like to be a brick. Fundamentally "an organism has conscious mental states if and only if there is something that it is like to *be* that organism – something it is like *for* the organism". This is "the subjective character of experience", which he maintained "is not captured by any of the familiar, recently devised reductive analyses of the mental, for all of them are logically compatible with its absence" (1974: 166). In this chapter we will start by examining his reasoning, then consider some further objections to physicalism.

4.1 Nagel's argument

Nagel chooses the example of bats because although they seem to be subjects of conscious experience they are also alien – especially the ones which perceive by echolocation. Although there is *something* it is like to be a bat, we have no idea of its character. Suppose we knew exactly how a bat works: all the details of its physiology, so that as a purely physical system it lay open to our view. Would that tell us what it was like for the bat to perceive the world by means of its echolocatory sense?

Because physiology includes no expressions for describing the character of experience, the answer is surely No. Even a complete physical account of the bat's workings wouldn't tell us what its experiences were like. Would such a physical account even provide us with a suitable basis for finding out what the bat's experiences were like for it? According to Nagel the answer is again No.

His reason is that in order to tell what it is like for the bat we should have to be able to acquire, or at least to approach, the bat's own *point of view*. The chief feature of an organism's point of view, he suggests, is that it endows it with a range of experiences of certain characteristic types. Because all normal human beings share the same sensory capacities, we share the same point of view and can have a good idea of what other people's experiences are like. In that sense facts about the experiences of other human beings are *accessible* to us, at least on occasions. But because bats have radically different sensory equipment we lack the capacity to have experiences like theirs. According to Nagel this means that we can form no conception of the bat's point of view, and so can never come to know what its experiences are like for it. Sometimes he calls the features which constitute there being "something it is like" for a creature the "phenomenological features of experience". He claims that facts about the phenomenological features of the experiences of bats are *inaccessible* to us – though presumably they would be accessible to other bats provided they were intelligent enough.

Nagel makes a broad distinction between "objective" facts, which are accessible in principle to any intelligent creature, and "subjective" facts, which are not. Among objective facts, we can take it, are facts about the shape and size of the earth. If bats were intelligent and interested enough they could discover such facts for themselves. But subjective facts, notably facts about what a creature's experiences are like, are accessible only to those who share the same point of view.

We are now in a position to grasp his objection to physicalism. He points out that physical theory is essentially *objective*. It self-consciously aims to capture only what is in principle available to intelligent beings regardless of their points of view. For that reason it seems impossible for it to account for subjective facts. His reasoning is encapsulated in the following remarks:

(N) If physicalism is to be defended, the phenomenological features must themselves be given a physical account. But when we examine their subjective character it seems that such a result is impossible. The reason is that every subjective phenomenon is essentially connected with a single point of view, and it seems inevitable that an objective, physical theory will abandon that point of view. (1974: 167)

4.2 Crucial ambiguities

How strong is that objection to physicalism? First let us try to get clearer about the distinction between "objective" facts (accessible from any point of view) and "subjective" facts (accessible only from a certain point of view). (It is intended only to be a broad distinction, so although you might easily think of various hard cases which might raise difficulties, they would be beside the point.)

We need to consider what should be counted as facts in this context. One suggestion is that facts are true propositions; another is that they are what make propositions true. Suppose for argument's sake that facts are true propositions. Then, since it is a commonplace that we can know *that* a proposition is true without grasping it, there seems no reason why we shouldn't be able to have access to "subjective" facts about the experiences of bats at least in this sense: that we can know whether or not the propositions expressing those facts are true or false. In this sense a person blind from birth can know that ripe tomatoes both are red and look red. But that can hardly trouble Nagel: by "access" to a fact he can't mean anything which falls short of *understanding* the corresponding true proposition. What, then, about the suggestion that the fact is not the true proposition itself, but whatever it is that makes it true? The trouble now is that what makes true a proposition about what an experience is like may well be objective, physical facts. To assume that such facts could not possibly be what made propositions about experiences true would be begging the question. So if Nagel's point depends on a distinction between subjective and objective facts, it starts to look problematic.

However, the key to the value of Nagel's distinction between subjective and objective facts is in effect a distinction between two kinds of *concepts*. We can distinguish roughly between what can be called "viewpoint-neutral" concepts and "viewpoint-relative" concepts. Viewpoint-neutral concepts are ones which could in principle be acquired by intelligent creatures of any species regardless of their point of view. They are the concepts in terms of which Nagel's objective facts would standardly be stated, and they include the concepts of physics and other natural sciences. Viewpoint-relative concepts, on the other hand, can be acquired only by creatures with an appropriate point of view: an appropriate set of sensory capacities. Such concepts would arguably include, for example, those of *red*, *sour*, *screeching*, *musty*. For it is at least plausible to say that only creatures capable of actually seeing red, tasting sour things, hearing screeching sounds, or smelling musty smells – or at least only creatures capable of imaginatively constructing such experiences – are capable of a full grasp of those concepts. In those terms Nagel can maintain that to the extent that facts depend on concepts, objective facts are accessible to all kinds of intelligent creatures because they are statable in terms of viewpoint-neutral concepts, while subjective facts are accessible only to creatures with points of view appropriate for the concepts needed for stating them. (There are further problems associated with these ideas, but we can ignore them for our purposes.)

We must surely accept that physics deals in facts statable in terms of viewpoint-neutral concepts, while the facts of subjective experience have to be stated in viewpoint-relative terms. But does it follow, as Nagel concludes in the passage quoted above, (N), that physicalism cannot give an "account" of the phenomenological features? Certainly he is right to say that "If physicalism is to be defended, the phenomenological features must themselves be given a physical account." Physicalists can't just pack up and go home once they have stated an identity thesis or a supervenience thesis; as we have seen, they must remove the perplexity that makes it so difficult to understand how a physical system can be a conscious subject. But must the explanation *itself* be in purely physical terms? Why? Provided physicalists can make clear in *some* way how a physical system can be a conscious subject, there seem to be no a priori constraints on the terms in which they do it.

How does Nagel's argument look in the light of these further considerations? Does the fact that physical theory is expressed in viewpoint-neutral terms prevent physicalists from explaining how a purely physical system can be a conscious subject? Suppose we concede the following premises to Nagel:

(N1) Physicalism must give an account of the "phenomenological features".
(N2) Physical theory is expressed in terms of viewpoint-neutral concepts.
(N3) The phenomenological features cannot be expressed in terms of viewpoint-neutral concepts.

It is difficult to resist (N1)–(N3). The question is whether they warrant the conclusion Nagel wants to draw, which is:

(C) Physicalism cannot give an account of the phenomenological features.

Examination of (N1)–(N3) reveals that (C) does not follow without some additional premise. For it is consistent with (N1)–(N3) that the account that physicalists have to provide should not itself have to *use* viewpoint-relative concepts – that it should not have to *describe* what it is like for the organisms in question. If his argument is to be valid it needs a further premise. The following would do the trick:

(N4) The physicalists' account of the phenomenological features must describe *what it is like* for the organisms it deals with to have whatever experiences they do have.

But why should physicalists concede anything like (N4)? They would have to concede it, of course, if any satisfactory account of the subjective character of conscious experience must say *what it is like* for whatever organisms it is about. But if the considerations noted in the last section have any force, no such account of the subjective character of experience is possible. In order to say what it is actually like for the creatures in question, the account must use viewpoint-relative concepts. Nagel himself has given persuasive reasons for thinking that in general no kind of creature (such as human beings) can grasp concepts dependent on the viewpoint of a radically alien type of creature (such as bats). But if an account of the nature of subjective conscious experience must satisfy (N4), *no* such account is possible: it is not even possible for dualists.

There is therefore no good reason why physicalists or anyone else should concede (N4), and there is a good reason (supplied by Nagel himself) to reject it. Certainly a physicalistic account of the nature of conscious experience must explain how it is possible for a purely physical system to be a conscious subject – something it is like something to be. But it cannot additionally be required to explain, for any arbitrary organism, what it is like for that organism. So it looks as if Nagel's objection to physicalism fails.

However, that conclusion must be qualified. Nagel has provided a powerful reason to reject *some* versions of physicalism: in particular, those strongly reductionist versions according to which psychological statements are either translatable into physical language, or in some other way state in physical terms what it is like for the creatures concerned to have the experiences they do have. That need not worry minimal physicalists, since earlier we noticed reasons why physicalists are not compelled to be reductionists in any non-trivial sense. Nagel's reasoning does not seem to be a serious threat to other forms of physicalism.

4.3 Jackson's "argument from knowledge"

Frank Jackson (1982) has developed a strand of Nagelian reasoning so that it appears to constitute a distinct objection to physicalism. His example is of a superb scientist Mary, who has normal vision but has been kept from birth in a colourless environment. From books and black and white television she has acquired a complete knowledge of all the physical and physiological facts about colour vision, together with all the relevant facts about causal relationships, evolutionary functions and so on – all characterized in "objective" terms, in Nagel's sense.

One day she is released from her grey prison: for the first time she sees colours. Immediately she learns something new – or so it seems. She learns *what it is like* to see the blue sky, red tomatoes, green grass. So it seems she acquires new information. Jackson maintains that this information goes beyond what Mary could have gleaned from the objective physical and functional facts. But if physicalism were true, he argues, there would be no such fresh information to be had. He concludes that physicalism is false.

Here is one way of setting out this "knowledge argument".

(J1)   Before Mary is released she knows all the relevant "objective" physical and functional facts about colour vision, together with whatever relevant further knowledge follows from that knowledge.   [Assumption]
(J2)   However, before she is released there is something about colour vision which Mary does not know; for example she does not know what it is like to see red tomatoes.
                                                                [Assumption]
(J3)   Therefore there is some knowledge about colour vision which is not physical or otherwise "objective", nor entailed by such knowledge.   [(J1) and (J2)]
(J4)   But if physicalism is true, then all knowledge is entailed by physical or otherwise "objective" knowledge.   [Assumption]
(J5)   Therefore physicalism is false.   [(J3) and (J4)]

4.4 Critique of the knowledge argument

The argument is impressive. It certainly appears to be valid; so physicalists had better find something wrong with one of its premises (J1), (J2) and (J4). Ever since 1982, when Jackson's article first appeared, they have had a happy time challenging this or that premise. In addition there has been a complaint that the argument depends on failing to take account of different senses of "knowledge".

One sample of this last objection is that when Mary comes to "know" what it is like to see red things, her knowledge is not the same sort of thing as factual knowledge but involves certain *abilities,* such as the ability to recognize instances of red when seen (see for example Nemirow 1980, Lewis 1983). Another objection, orthogonal to the first, is that when Mary sees red tomatoes for the first time she acquires a new "perspective" – a "first-person" perspective – on information she already has (see for example P. M. Churchland 1985; Horgan 1984; Tye 1986). Now, we have no reason to suppose that what premise (J1) takes to be Mary's possession of purely factual knowledge about colour vision should automatically provide her with either special abilities or a new perspective. If that is right, there is no inconsistency in premise (J1)-type knowledge failing to cover premise (J2)-type knowledge, in which case (J3) doesn't follow from those premises. If any such objection is sound, the argument as a whole rests on a fallacy of equivocation.

A different approach taken by some physicalists, notably Dennett, is to maintain that if Mary really does know all the physical and "objective" truths about colour vision, then she also knows, or at any rate could eventually work out, *what it is like* to see red things, green things and so on. It would take imagination and hard work, but could still be done (Dennett 1991: 399–401).

We saw earlier that physicalists can consistently agree with Nagel's line about viewpoint-relative concepts. They can accept that many concepts by which we characterize our conscious experiences cannot be fully grasped except by those who can adopt a certain point of view. So long as Mary is imprisoned in her grey world, she cannot have the sorts of experiences that would enable her to grasp human colour concepts fully. So she cannot (*pace* Dennett) come to know what it is like to see red and other colours. Her purely theoretical knowledge doesn't actually give her either those experiences, or the imaginative know-how to construct them.

However, that doesn't mean Mary can't work out *which sentences describing colour experiences are true.* She can. For she knows in what circumstances English speakers use colour words. She also knows in what circumstances she would use them. She, like the others, would describe ripe tomatoes as "red", fresh grass as "green", and so on. And she knows all the physics and physiology involved in explaining how the surfaces of things interact with human visual systems. Given detailed information about some object, therefore, she could work out which colour it was. Hence she can work out which sentences such as "This berry is red" are strictly implied by the totality of purely physical truths P. The trouble is just that her grasp of the key concepts is not quite as full as that of those who have had the necessary kinds of experiences.

So there is a sense in which she lacks a full understanding of just which truths such sentences express. It is only when she emerges into the world of full colour that she is able to acquire that understanding. By filling in the gaps in her experience, knowing what she is doing, she fills in the gaps in her grasp of the colour concepts.

If that approach is right, then the argument from knowledge is no threat to the *minimal* physicalism expressed by theses (SI.1)–(SI.3) explained in Chapter 3. Minimal physicalists can accept premises (J1) and (J4) of the knowledge argument on the understanding that the knowledge they apply to is purely theoretical. But they will point out that (J2) is true only if the knowledge Mary is said to acquire requires something beyond merely theoretical knowledge: specifically, it requires the knower to have had certain kinds of experiences. And that, of course, demolishes the argument. (There is still a controversy about the diagnosis of the argument. See Dennett 1991: 398–401; Kirk 1994: 226–31; Tye 1995: 171–8.)

4.5 "Transposed qualia"

Do you see the world as I do? In particular, do you see colours as I see them? Of course one of us might be colour blind; but there are tests for that, and the difference would eventually show up. An intriguing possibility is that you and I should both pass all possible tests for colour discrimination yet still experience colours in two different ways. The experiences you have when we are both seeing ripe tomatoes in normal conditions might be like the ones I should have if the tomatoes were unripe, and vice versa. This is the alleged possibility of "transposed qualia" (in this particular case, "inverted spectrum"). Since the different hues stand in certain relations of relative closeness and difference (red is closer to orange than it is to green, for example), the differences would be detectable unless those relations were preserved. So the differences would have to apply to other colours than red and green; they would have to run systematically through the rest of the colour solid. Before we consider this suggestion, we need to take note of the jargon of "qualia".

The particular character of a conscious experience – of the blue of the sky, the smell of roasting coffee beans, the sound of a tenor saxophone – is sometimes referred to as a "phenomenal quality (or property)", or a "quale". ("Quale" is Latin neuter singular; "qualia" is plural). Qualia are usually thought of as properties of the experiences themselves; it is also possible to think of them as properties of the subject of the experiences, although nothing here turns on this detail. The idea of spectrum inversion is a neat illustration of the qualia idea, since it seems particularly easy to imagine. However, there is a crucial difference between the way dualists conceive of qualia and the way physicalists conceive of them (assuming they don't, like Dennett, want to eliminate them altogether).

The crucial point is that dualists conceive of qualia as non-physical, hence as separable from the purely physical workings of the organism – in theory if not in nature as it actually is. For dualists, the possibility which matters is that any of us could have had *exactly the same* underlying physical structures but different qualia. However, as we saw earlier (Ch. 3, §3.11), physicalists are committed to the view that what makes mental descriptions true, and what mental descriptions therefore apply to, is purely physical. If, therefore, exactly the same physical facts were compatible with different types of colour experiences, the strict implication thesis, and with it physicalism, would be false. So physicalists are committed to the falsity of the transposed qualia possibility as conceived by dualists. Physicalists can still concede a different version of the thesis: one according to which qualia differences, though behaviourally undetectable, are underlain by hidden physical differences (Shoemaker 1975, 1981b; Kirk 1994).

Can physicalists refute the possibility alleged by dualists? One uncompromising response is behaviourism, to be discussed in Chapter 5. If behaviourism is true, then the behavioural undetectability of the alleged experiential differences is logically sufficient to guarantee that in reality there are no such differences at all. But behaviourism is a shaky support here, since the inverted spectrum idea is often regarded as an objection to it. The same applies if physicalists appeal to verificationism. If the meaningfulness of what we say depends on the possibility of discovering whether or not it is true, then the idea of transposed qualia without physical differences is meaningless: the alleged differences would be impossible to discover. However, enthusiasts for transposed qualia will insist that the idea is perfectly intelligible, in which case it is an objection to verificationist assumptions as well as to behaviourism. A more promising strategy for physicalists is to challenge the assumption that qualia are logically detachable from physical processes in the first place. I will pursue that suggestion below (§§4.10, 4.11). Here I will say a little more to explain the appeal of the alleged trans- posed qualia possibility.

A favourite argument starts from a situation like this. Anna wakes up one morning to find that – as it seems – the colours of things have suddenly been transposed. Fresh grass and unripe tomatoes look red to her, blood and unripe tomatoes look green, and so on. Since no one else has had the same shocking experience, it seems to be a change not in the colours of things, but in the way she sees them. In time, to avoid confusion, she comes to agree with others' descriptions; and after a further interval she comes to forget the sudden switch altogether and becomes indistinguishable from someone with normal colour vision. Yet, so defenders of the transposed qualia idea maintain, Anna really continues to see things in the new way. They add that this sort of thought-experiment shows that qualia are indeed logically detachable from whatever physical processes underlie them.

There are all kinds of ingenious variations on this scenario. One that I personally like has the subject – me for example – seeing colours relatively transposed *with different eyes*. With my left eye shut and the right one open I see colours in one way; with my right eye shut and the left one open I see colours another way. It is tempt- ing to conclude that there can be no absolutely necessary connec- tion from the physical set-up in my brain and my seeing colours in one of these two ways rather than the other – but as usual, what it is easy to conclude is not necessarily correct. I leave it as an exercise for the reader to determine whether these stories are valuable thought-experiments or treacherous "intuition pumps". (For – highly – critical discussion see for example Dennett 1991: 389–98.)

4.6 Zombies

The idea of transposed qualia makes vivid the nagging question of why a given physical structure should result in one particular way of experiencing the world rather than any of an apparently unlimited number of alternative ways: why is it like *this* rather than some other way? The notion of "zombies" is a way of making vivid the companion to that question: why should a purely physical structure result in any sort of conscious experience at all: why is it like *anything* rather than nothing?

These philosophical zombies are very different from the zombies of Haitian folklore. Voodoo zombies, I understand, are corpses caused by sorcerers to walk about and work, perhaps also to talk. But as horror films suggest, they don't look or behave like normal living people. Philosophical zombies look and behave *exactly* like normal living people. To get clear about this idea, imagine that somewhere in this or another world there is an exact physical double of yourself. It not only looks and behaves like you, it matches you in every detail of body and brain: it is a particle-for-particle duplicate. The assumption is that this "zombie twin" is a purely physical system, and that the workings of its nervous system and the rest of its body ensure that it is in all observable respects indistinguishable from you. If you discuss the mind–body problem, so does it – as far as we can tell. The only difference is that it lacks any sort of inner life. It is *defined* as having no conscious experiences at all, no qualia. Are such things possible?

By now the point of that question will probably be clear. Even minimal physicalists are committed to all psychological truths being strictly implied by P. *If* zombies are so much as a "logical" possibility (that is, involve no contradiction or incoherence: see §1.5), then mental truths are *not* strictly implied by P. In that case physicalism is false. The bare or logical possibility of zombies would disprove physicalism. Maintaining that zombies are so much as barely possible thus commits you to at least two highly significant theses. One is common to parallelism, epiphenomenalism and physicalism: that human behaviour – in the sense of bodily movements – is explicable in purely physical terms. The other is dualistic: that human consciousness involves something beyond the physical. By uniting these two theses the zombie idea neatly encapsulates a fundamental problem in the philosophy of mind. (Joseph Levine regards it as a symptom of what he calls the "explanatory gap": roughly, the difficulty or perhaps the impossibility of explaining how it is that physical processes give rise to qualia: Levine 2001.)

It is undeniable that zombies *seem* to be at any rate barely possible. David Chalmers says, "I have a clear picture of what I am conceiving when I conceive of a zombie". To him the possibility just seems "obvious" (1996, 99). Even after long reflection the possibility can still seem genuine; and many philosophers agree with Chalmers. Physicalists therefore face a serious problem. How, if at all, can they show that zombies are *not* even barely possible? Before considering attempts to do that, let us examine some *arguments* for the possibility of zombies. For everyone agrees that the mere fact that we think we can imagine a particle-for-particle duplicate of a living human being without conscious experiences does not prove it is a genuine possibility. We can imagine that the ratio of a circle's circumference to its diameter is represented exactly by some rational number, say 13/4; but that doesn't prove it might *be* a rational number; and in fact we know that necessarily π is not rational. So what arguments are there for the possibility of zombies?

4.7 The "conceivability argument"
Chalmers uses a "conceivability argument". It goes as follows:

(C1)   Zombies are conceivable.
(C2)   Whatever is conceivable is possible.
(C3)   Therefore zombies are possible.

Clearly this argument is valid. However, both premises are unclear as stated, and controversial even when they have been clarified. Evidently the question of how we should understand "conceivable" in this context is crucial.

Many philosophers would concede that zombies are conceivable in *some* sense, for it is often assumed that there are no a priori links between the concepts involved. Christopher Hill, for example, claims "there are no substantive a priori ties between the concept of pain and the concept of C-fiber stimulation" on the ground that "it is in principle possible to master either of these concepts fully without having mastered the other" (1997: 76. Papineau makes a similar assumption: 2002: 49). However, in that very liberal sense it is "conceivable" that the ratio of a circle's circumference to its diameter should be exactly 13/4, which we know it isn't. So if premise (C1) is understood in that sense it is indisputably true. The trouble is that, by the same token, premise (C2) is indisputably false when understood in that liberal sense. The fact that it is conceivable in *that* sense that the circumference:diameter ratio should be a rational number does not entail that it is possible, since it has actually been mathematically proved to be impossible. Nor would it help to say that the sense of "possible" could be modified in line with the liberal sense of "conceivable" so as to ensure that (C2) came out true after all. That would provide a sense of "possible" that was obviously too weak to do what seems to be the main philosophical work of the idea of zombies: refuting physicalism (see §§3.10, 3.11).

Evidently, then, the lower the threshold for conceivability, the easier it is to accept (C1) – but the harder it is to accept (C2). It therefore seems that very strong conditions must be imposed on what is to count as conceivability for premises (C1) and (C2).

Chalmers has characterized the required sense of "conceivability" as "ideal conceivability, or conceivability on ideal rational reflection" (1999: 477). This is an epistemic notion he has since refined in terms of a fairly intricate taxonomy of notions of conceivability (2002a). The most important for our purposes seems to be what he calls "ideal positive conceivability". A situation is "positively" conceivable if we can imagine it not only coherently, but in such a way that arbitrary details can be filled in without any contradiction revealing itself. A situation is "ideally" positively conceivable "when its positive conceivability cannot be undermined on idealized reflection". This last idea is further explained by saying that "it must be possible in principle to flesh out any missing details of an imagined situation that verifies" the statement of possibility in question, so that "these details are imagined clearly and distinctly and . . . no contradiction is revealed". It "must also be the case that arbitrary rational reflection on the imagined situation will not undermine the interpretation of the imagined situation as one in which [that situation] is the case" (2002a: 153).

With some sort of grasp of what is meant by "conceivable" as it occurs in the conceivability argument, we now face two key questions. One is: if zombies are conceivable, does it follow that they are possible? The other is: are zombies conceivable? Only if the answer to each question is Yes will the conceivability argument succeed. Let us take them in that order.

4.8 Does conceivability entail possibility?

Is "ideal positive conceivability" strong enough to ensure that if zombies are conceivable, they are possible? Chalmers himself finds the logical possibility of zombies "obvious". He remarks that "it certainly seems that a coherent situation is described; I can discern no contradiction in the description". He goes on to say that the burden of proof is on those who claim a given description is logically impossible. "If no reasonable analysis of the terms in question points toward a contradiction, or even makes the existence of a contradiction plausible, then there is a natural assumption in favor of logical possibility" (1996: 96; see also Chalmers 1999).

Those claims are disputed. It is argued that the epistemic question of what is or appears to be conceivable is not generally a reliable guide to possibility, and that there are special factors at work in the psycho-physical case which have a strong tendency to mislead us. For example, it is urged that what enables us to imagine or conceive of states of consciousness is a different cognitive faculty from what enables us to conceive of physical facts: "there are significant differences between the cognitive factors responsible for Cartesian intuitions [such as the intuition that zombies are logically possible] and those responsible for modal intuitions of a wide variety of other kinds" (Hill and McLaughlin 1999: 449; see also Hill 1997). This attack brings with it a challenge to the assumption that the burden of proof is on those who deny the zombie possibility. Another relevant consideration is the stringency of the constraints on ideal positive conceivability. Recall that, for an imagined situation to be conceivable in this sense, it is required that no amount of rational reflection on it will bring a contradiction to light, or reveal it as ultimately incoherent. Now, those who deny the logical possibility of zombies do not have to concede that it will be easy to explain exactly why they are not possible. They can insist that the nature of consciousness is extremely hard to understand, and that what strikes some people as obviously possible might eventually be revealed as contradictory or incoherent (see for example T. Nagel 1998).

Of course Chalmers is aware of the objection that there might be a hidden incoherence in the zombie idea. He replies that "the only route available to an opponent here is to claim that in describing the zombie world as a zombie world, we are misapplying the concepts, and that in fact there is a conceptual contradiction lurking in the description", and goes on to repeat that he can "detect no internal incoherence" (1996: 99). Below we will first examine his arguments for the conceivability of zombies, then some arguments against.

4.9 For the conceivability of zombies

In his most systematic defence of the zombie idea Chalmers (1996) assembles a series of five arguments for the conceivability of zombies. Two we have already discussed: Jackson's knowledge argument and the idea of transposed qualia. Chalmers has three more.

The first argument can be put as follows. Consider a population of homunculi who deactivate your brain and arrange to take over its functions while keeping the rest of your body in working order (this idea comes from Block 1980). They organize themselves so that they function isomorphically to the components of your brain, each person playing the part of a single neurone. Some receive signals from the afferent nerve endings of your body and transmit them to colleagues; others receive signals from colleagues and transmit them to your efferent nerves; most receive and send signals to colleagues (perhaps by mobile phone) exactly as your own neurones do. Now, would such a system be conscious? Intuitively one may be inclined to say "Obviously not". Some would bite the bullet and answer "Yes". However, it is crucial that the present argument does not depend on assuming that the system would *not* be conscious. It depends only on the assumption that its not being conscious involves no contradiction, an assumption many people find reasonable. In Chalmers's words, all that matters here is that when we say the system might lack consciousness,

> a meaningful possibility is being expressed, and it is an open question whether consciousness arises or not . . . From these cases it follows that the existence of my conscious experience is not logically entailed by the facts about my functional organi-
> zation.   (1996: 97)

Possibly, then – as we might suppose for argument's sake – the system is not conscious. But if it isn't, then it is already very much like a zombie. The only difference is that it has little people where a zombie has neurones. But why should that make a relevant difference? Why should switching from homunculi to neurones necessarily switch on the light of consciousness? "For it is clear", Chalmers says, "that there is no more of a conceptual entailment from biochemistry to consciousness than there is from . . . a group of homunculi" (1996: 97).

In spite of the appeal of that argument, physicalists will point out that it depends entirely on the assumption that there is no contradiction in supposing the homunculus-head lacks consciousness. They do not seem compelled to concede that assumption. Of course it can appear at first sight that no contradiction is involved, but since we are now thinking in terms of "ideal positive conceivability" we have to be sure that rational reflection will never turn up considerations to the contrary. Thus the claim that such cases show that "the existence of my conscious experience is not logically entailed by the facts about my functional organization" is not as well justified as may at first appear. (See also §§6.6, 8.11.)

A second argument appeals to an alleged "epistemic asymmetry in knowledge of consciousness" (Chalmers 1996: 102). The idea is that our knowledge of consciousness comes from first-person experience, not from observation of things in the external world. This contrasts with all our other knowledge of reality. Chalmers makes two important claims in this connection. One is that:

> Even if we knew every last detail about the physics of the universe – the configuration, causation, and evolution among all the fields and particles in the spatial manifold – *that* information would not lead us to postulate the existence of conscious experience. (1996: 101)

Leave aside the question whether that claim is true; the question is whether it is relevant. What matters after all is not whether knowing the purely physical facts would *necessarily* lead us to suppose there is consciousness. It is whether consciousness actually does logically supervene on those facts. And now the point is that it might supervene even if knowing the facts didn't automatically lead the knowers to postulate it. The claim therefore doesn't seem relevant.

Chalmers's last argument is "from the absence of analysis". He rightly says that his opponents "will have to give us some idea of how the existence of consciousness might be entailed by the physical facts", but says that "any attempt to demonstrate such an entailment is doomed to failure" (1996: 104). In support of that assertion he urges first that the only "remotely tenable" type of analysis of consciousness is a functional one (something to be investigated in Ch. 6); and secondly, that no functional analysis could do the job. In particular he says that what makes states conscious "is that they have a certain phenomenal feel, and this feel is not something that can be functionally defined away" (1996: 105). However, we know that what seems to be the case "on the face of it" is not decisive. There are various possible replies to Chalmers's objection. Rather than anticipate them at this stage I will put off further consideration of Chalmers's argument until Chapters 6 and 8.

4.10 Against the conceivability of zombies

When you first encounter the idea it may seem comparatively easy to conceive of zombies. But that appearance starts to fade when you recall that conceivability requires no contradiction or incoherence to be revealed even under "arbitrary rational reflection". The zombie idea entails that human beings are compounds of fully functioning purely physical bodies plus non-physical causally inert qualia. Reflection on this view of normal human consciousness reveals what are, at the very least, serious difficulties. Daniel Dennett thinks those who accept the possibility of zombies have failed to imagine them thoroughly. They have failed to consider deeply enough how the relations between consciousness and physical events should be conceived. Consciousness, he suggests, is "not a single wonderful separable thing . . . but a huge complex of many different informational capacities that individually arise for a wide variety of reasons . . . it is not a separate organ or a separate medium or a separate talent" (1995: 324). He compares *health*:

> Supposing that by an act of stipulative imagination you can remove consciousness while leaving all cognitive systems intact – a quite standard but entirely bogus feat of imagination – is like supposing that by an act of stipulative imagination, you can

> remove health while leaving all bodily functions and powers intact ... Health isn't that sort of thing, and neither is consciousness. (1995: 325)

The point that consciousness is not a separable thing is enormously important if true. That is why the zombie idea is so useful: it highlights a particular way of conceiving of the relation between conscious experience and physical processes. If it is correct, then the relation between qualia and physical facts becomes extremely mysterious, as we shall see shortly.

A more familiar difficulty, which we noted in connection with epiphenomenalism, is that the zombie idea makes it at best extremely hard to understand how we can think or talk *about* our experiences (see §2.9). Imagine my zombie twin says, "Mm! Roasting coffee beans: I love that smell!" That utterance cannot be explained by reference to his experiences because by definition he has none; it has to be explained purely in terms of physical processes. But if that is true of my zombie twin, my own identical utterance is similarly explicable in terms of physical processes – when these are assumed by the friends of zombies neither to be identical with conscious experiences nor to constitute them. If you asked me to explain my utterance of "Mm! Roasting coffee beans!", I would mention this delicious olfactory experience. But if the zombie idea is sound that would be a mistake: the actual experience, the supposedly non-physical "quale", had nothing to do with causing me to mention it. At most it was related to that behaviour as a joint effect of some common physical cause. So for the friends of zombies "it seems that consciousness is explanatorily irrelevant to our claims and judgments about consciousness" (1996: 177).

That is strongly counter-intuitive. Many people see it as sufficient by itself to rule out the possibility of zombies; they think we know that what we think and say about qualia is partly caused by those qualia themselves. The problem is magnified if knowing something, or being able to refer to it, requires us to be causally affected by it. Many philosophers accept such causal conditions on knowledge and reference; but the friends of zombies must reject them on pain of absurdity. They could not even state their position if they neither knew nor even referred to their experiences.

Chalmers offers a solution to what for him is a "paradox": the "paradox of phenomenal judgment". On his account the situations of zombies and ourselves are radically different because we are "acquainted" with our experiences. This "intimate epistemic relation" to our experiences both ensures that we can refer to them and justifies our claims to know about them. Since our zombie twins have no experiences, their quasi-phenomenal judgements are unjustified. But Chalmers suggests that even though qualia have no causal influence on our judgements, their mere presence partially *constitutes* the contents of the thoughts involved: it helps to ensure that our thoughts are about those qualia. It also, he thinks, constitutes justification for our knowledge claims even when our experiences are not explanatorily relevant to making the judgements involved (1996: 172–209; see also Chalmers 2000b).

That suggestion might quieten some worries, but it leaves others untouched. The main difficulty can be put roughly like this. The zombie idea implies that each of us consists of a body somehow associated with non-physical, causally inert qualia. These qualia may be caused by processes in the body; but they themselves have no physical effects. The question arises of how such qualia could make the intimate contribution that our conscious experiences actually make to our lives. More fundamentally, there has to be some explanation of how, in spite of being so detached, they have *anything to do with our consciousness at all*. On closer examination it looks as if the zombie idea makes it impossible to explain that.

4.11 Apparent incoherence of the zombie idea

To see why, let us start by considering my zombie twin. The difference between him and me is that he has no qualia while I have lots. So suppose that somehow he suddenly acquires a full set of these non-physical qualia. Does that make him conscious? Curiously enough it doesn't make *him* conscious because by definition he is a purely physical system and – given the assumption that all physical events are physically caused – cannot be affected by anything non-physical. Qualia no more affect him than they affect the coins in his pocket. Now, the friends of zombies will insist that this is beside the point because a human being is not a mere body, but a compound consisting of a body together with qualia. The qualia that my zombie twin suddenly acquires are supposed to be *his:* they are non-physical properties of that particular physical system, not of some other system. The difficulty now is this: *how could they be his in any sense that matters?* How could they result in the existence of a conscious subject? Modifying my zombie twin in other ways – dyeing his hair green, for example – wouldn't transform him into a conscious subject. Why should equipping him with a bunch of qualia do the trick?

The point of these questions emerges when we think about our abilities to distinguish, compare and attend to our qualia. These abilities require us to be both sensitive to qualia and able to process information about them. But the zombie idea seems to leave no room for us to have both of these features. Certainly the body can perform the relevant cognitive functions, such as storing information; but it cannot be sensitive to non-physical qualia because by definition qualia have no effects on it. And qualia cannot perform *either* of those functions. They cannot distinguish or compare qualia because distinguishing and comparing are cognitive activities, while a quale is an inert phenomenal quality incapable of cognition. (Qualia cannot store information, which any sort of cognition requires.) Nor are qualia sensitive to qualia, since that would require them to be affected by them, which they are not (as follows from their definition).

Of course it would be fallacious to conclude, just because neither qualia nor bodies are sensitive to qualia or capable of comparing them, that a body plus qualia cannot do those things. A piece of string isn't a candle; a piece of wax isn't a candle; but string enclosed in wax *constitutes* a candle. The friends of zombies might argue analogously, and insist that a functioning human body plus appropriate qualia constitutes a conscious subject: no *causal* sensitivity to qualia is necessary. (That would be to apply to this problem Chalmers's solution to the "paradox of phenomenal judgment" noted above: having and being justified in having beliefs about qualia is secured on his account by the mere presence of appropriate qualia when the right brain processes are going on.)

However, you can't produce constitution by fiat. There must be an explanation of why putting qualia together with a body ensures that the result is a conscious subject; yet the materials for such an explanation do not seem to be available. The case of *attending* to qualia helps to illustrate this point. (It is worth noting that Chalmers's own account of "phenomenal" concepts is in terms of a subject attending to or demonstrating the quality of an experience: 2002b.) Attending is not just a matter of acquiring beliefs about whatever is attended to. Beliefs can arise without any activity by the subject; attending, in contrast, requires some kind of activity. More to the point: attending to something can *prompt* the acquisition of beliefs. Attending to my present coffee-smell quale, for example, may prompt me to compare it with the smell of the coffee I ground yesterday – and such comparing involves a fair amount of cognitive processing. It seems impossible to conceive how there should be prompting of that sort unless the quale has causal efficacy. How could I be said to be "attending" to the coffee-quale if it has no effects on the cognitive processes involved in my storing and processing information about it? The friends of zombies might reply that according to them qualia are properties of the subject. But the problem is to understand how the mere causation of qualia by physical processes in a body can provide for the existence of *something capable of comparing and attending to qualia*. Just asserting that the relevant qualia are "mine" is no help, for the reasons given above. Nor, of course, would it help to claim that these inert non-physical qualia are special basic properties that just have to be accepted as what make people conscious. That would be no better than appealing to magic.

The key points are these. The zombie idea entails that qualia are non-physical and have no effects on physical processes. But we can compare and attend to our qualia. That necessarily has effects on cognitive processing, which in turn depends on the brain's power to store information – that is, on physical processes. So there seems to be a contradiction. On the one hand we have to be able to compare and attend to our qualia. On the other hand this requires qualia to have effects on physical processes, contrary to the zombie idea.

It therefore looks as if the zombie idea depends on an incoherent conception of the mind, one which makes it impossible to understand how we could be conscious. However, the intuitions that feed the zombie idea remain powerful and alluring. Ideally, physicalists ought to be able to offer an account of consciousness capable of convincing reasonably objective judges, even if the victims of zombie fever remain resistant. We shall consider the main attempts to supply such an account in Chapter 8.

4.12 Conclusion

There are other objections to physicalism than those discussed in this chapter, some of which will be examined later. But the ones discussed here have struck many philosophers as particularly hard to deal with. What we all need is an explanation of what is involved in having mental states. One approach is behaviourism: the subject of Chapter 5.

Main points in Chapter 4

1. Nagel's objections to physicalism depend on distinguishing "objective" and "subjective" facts (§4.1).
2. It is useful to express his main points in terms of "viewpoint-neutral" and "viewpoint-relative" concepts. Physicalists are not compelled to "give an account of the phenomenological features" in such a way that they can describe the actual character of the experiences of the organisms they deal with (§§4.1, 4.2).
3. Analysis of Jackson's knowledge argument suggests it is no threat to the minimal physicalism of 3.11 above (§§4.3, 4.4).
4. Physicalists have various possible replies to the inverted spectrum objection (§4.5).
5. The idea of zombies encapsulates a real problem for physicalism (§4.6).
6. But the "conceivability argument" and other arguments for the logical possibility of zombies are not compelling; and the conception it implies of the relation between qualia and physical processes appears on close inspection to be unintelligible (§§4.7–4.11).

Further reading

Nagel's classic presentation of his reasoning is in Nagel (1974). See also Nagel (1986). For discussions, see, for example, Dennett (1991: 441–8) and Kirk (1994: 218–26).

Jackson's "argument from knowledge" is presented in Jackson (1982). For discussion, see, for example, P. M. Churchland (1985), Dennett (1991: 399–401), Horgan (1984), Kirk (1994: 226–31), Lewis (1983) and Nemirow (1980).

The inverted spectrum is discussed in Chalmers (1996: *passim*), Kirk (1981, 1994) and Shoemaker (1975, 1981b).

For zombies see Chalmers (1996) (for), Kirk (1974) (for) and Kirk (1994, 1999) (against). See also Block (1978, 1995) and Dennett (1995).

For conceivability and conceivability arguments see Chalmers (1996, 1999, 2002a), other papers in Gendler & Hawthorne (eds) (2002), Hill (1997), Hill & McLaughlin (1999), Levine (2001) and T. Nagel (1998).

5 Behaviourism

The challenge is to provide a satisfying account of how a purely physical system can have mental states. Behind that stands the wider challenge of explaining *what it is* to be a subject of mental states. Behaviourism is a tremendously influential approach to meeting those challenges.

Behaviourism in psychology was a methodological project aimed at making psychology scientific. Attempts in the nineteenth and early twentieth centuries to do that by basing psychological laws on people's reports of their experiences had run into the sand, partly because of the difficulty of interpreting the reports. The new idea was that it ought to be possible to arrive at laws relating publicly observable facts about sensory inputs and behavioural outputs, without bothering about what experimental subjects had to say (although of course their reports themselves could be treated as just more behavioural outputs). This idea influenced philosophical thinking about psychology, resulting in philosophical behaviourism (I will usually omit "philosophical" from now on). In this chapter we shall examine some varieties of behaviourism, together with behaviouristically influenced ideas in general.

5.1 Behaviouristic reductionism

How do we know what other people are thinking or feeling? Often of course we don't know: people can be inscrutable or downright dishonest. But sometimes we do know. How? The obvious answer is that we can see what they do and hear what they say: we know on the basis of their behaviour. Behaviourists urge that instead of following Descartes and conceiving of the mind as if it were some kind of thing, we should conceive of expressions such as "the mind", "intelligence", "understanding", "emotion" and so on as ways of talking about behaviour and behavioural dispositions (how people *would* behave in various situations: see below). If they are right, and having mental states is just a matter of behaving and being disposed to behave in certain ways, then there is no great problem over how mind and body are related: all that is needed is a body capable of the right sorts of behaviour. Today, in spite of continuing uncertainty about how the brain works, there is little doubt that the physical processes of the human body *are* capable of producing the right sorts of behaviour. So if behaviourism is right, the mind–body problem is solved!

For many kinds of mental states behaviourism is appealing. Take two absolutely central types of mental states, recognized by all but the most hard-nosed eliminativists: beliefs and desires. Beliefs and desires have "intentionality". They have "content", they are "about" things; and beliefs, at any rate, can be true or false. Behaviourism offers valuable suggestions for explaining those features of beliefs and desires. What is it to believe there are whales living in the Atlantic? Well, if you have that belief and are asked "What creatures live in the Atlantic?" you will be disposed to reply "Whales"; asked where there are whales living, you will be disposed to say "In the Atlantic". Moving on to desires: what is it to want a cup of coffee? If you are near a coffee shop you may be disposed to go inside; if you are at home you will be disposed to go to the kitchen and prepare a cup; and so on. Similarly for intentions. If you intend to catch the next bus you will be disposed to get to the bus stop in time; disposed to watch out for your bus; and so on – while once you have finally caught the bus, those dispositions will lapse.

For sensations and experiences, in contrast, behaviourism seems grossly implausible. Consider what it says about pain. It says that if something harms us we acquire dispositions to wince, groan, or even scream, depending on the severity of the damage; and that we are disposed to lose those dispositions when a pain-killer is administered or after the wound has healed. So far we must all agree. But behaviourism adds that there is *no more* to pain than that. To have a toothache is to be disposed to say "Ow, that hurts!" if someone touches the affected jaw; to avoid chewing on that side of the mouth; to take aspirins; to go to the dentist. Now, although pains are certainly associated with such dispositions, we think of the pains as distinct from them. Indeed we find it natural to describe the pains as *causing* them, which would be nonsensical if they were nothing but those dispositions themselves.

An extreme variety of behaviourism was to the effect that statements about mental states are translatable in behavioural terms, or at least have logical equivalents in those terms. Given a psychological statement such as "Anna is miserable", "Bill believes it is raining", "Chris wants a cup of coffee", there was supposed to be an equivalent statement in terms of behaviour and behavioural dispositions. There are several difficulties over this project, but the decisive one is this. Behaviour is never determined by a single belief or desire or other individual mental state, but by the subject's total mental state at the time: all their desires, beliefs, feelings and other attitudes, as well as such factors as temperament, working together. If you live in a rainy climate and think it's going to rain, then you are likely to take an umbrella – because you don't want to get wet. But if you live in an arid climate and think it will rain, then far from taking an umbrella, you may leave your shirt off so as to enjoy the sensation of rain falling on your back. There seems to be no pattern of behaviour that would reflect that belief regardless of your other mental states. Similarly for desires and intentions.

You might suggest that there is at any rate one fairly reliable indicator: dispositions to produce *verbal* behaviour, or to react in some way to other people's verbal behaviour. As Carnap once put it, if "Q" is a psychological term, "Then the utterance by speaking or writing of the statement 'I am now . . . in the state Q' is (under suitable circumstances, e.g., as to reliability, etc.) an observable symptom for the state Q" (1938: 420). Unfortunately verbal behaviour seems to be as much subject to the general objection just noted as non-verbal behaviour. What you say, and whether you nod or shake your head in response to what others say, will depend on whether you are willing to let others know what you think or feel, or whether you want to mislead them. It is generally agreed that the project of finding a behavioural equivalent for each individual mental statement fails because individual mental states are never the sole determinants of behaviour.

5.2 Behavioural dispositions

We normally suppose there is a big difference between behaviour on the one hand, and thoughts and feelings on the other. Behaviour may or may not reveal thoughts and feelings; but we tend to assume that behaviour is one thing, actual mental states are something else. *Behaviourism undermines this assumption.* We have noted that behaviourists don't go so far as to say that mental states are just a matter of *actual* behaviour. It would be plainly false to suggest that every different psychological state is reflected in a different pattern of actual behaviour. After all, "Sometimes I sits and thinks, and sometimes I just sits." To deal with this difficulty behaviourism takes account not only of actual behaviour but of what the organism *would* do in different circumstances.

If a sugar-lump is placed in water, it dissolves. But some sugar-lumps never encounter any liquids. They are burnt up or pulverized, or otherwise destroyed. Yet they still have the *disposition* to dissolve: it remains true that they *would* dissolve *if* they were to be put in water. Sugar-lumps retain that disposition throughout their existence. But when we think of the behavioural dispositions that human beings have in connection with their mental states, not only is there a vast number, but some of them change, sometimes very rapidly. Certainly a person may permanently have a friendly disposition, as we say, or an envious one. But as we engage with the changing world around us we also acquire and lose a mass of fleeting dispositions relating to what we see, hear and otherwise perceive. Behaviourism can also legitimately appeal to the fact that we have dispositions to acquire and lose other dispositions in certain circumstances. I might be disposed to take my umbrella if I go out this afternoon having noted that the sky is very cloudy (that would be a "first-order" disposition); but I am also disposed to lose that disposition if I see the sky has cleared up (a "second-order" disposition). If I see a tiger coming down the road I might suddenly acquire a (first-order) disposition to stay indoors; if I see keepers capture it and take it away in a van I will lose that disposition – because I am (second-order) disposed to acquire and lose such dispositions in such circumstances.

Think of a computer running a complex program, such as one for train passengers which, when you give it your desired times and places of departure and arrival, prints out a rail route-plan. Its program endows the machine with a complex system of dispositions, including "higher-order" dispositions to acquire and lose other dispositions. *If* such-and-such a time and place is put in, *then* refer to such-and-such locations in memory and do so-and-so, *provided that* doing so-and-so satisfies condition C; otherwise do such-and-such; and so on. The program gives the railway computer a complex structure of dispositions. Reflecting on it we can get some idea of the sense in which mental states are said by behaviourists to consist of complexes of dispositions.

The behaviourist is not claiming that human behaviour is explicable purely in terms of "stimulus and response", or "inputs and outputs". The example of the complex computer program should make clear that in any case that would be a mistake. The effect of such a program is *not* to ensure that there is a set of possible inputs on the one hand, and a set of possible outputs on the other, such that for each of the possible inputs a particular one of the possible outputs is specified, and the machine's entire behaviour is explicable in those terms: in other words, the program is *not* a "look-up table". (That is the sort of system Descartes seems to have assumed to be the only kind a machine could instantiate.) On the contrary, a complex program is likely to be one where exactly the same input will result in different outputs depending on the machine's *internal* state, which changes over time. (Recall the finite automaton considered in §1.12.)

With those preliminary points in mind we can state a non-reductionistic version of behaviourism:

> There is no more to having mental states than having a complex of certain kinds of behavioural dispositions.

This is a "global" or "holistic" variety of behaviourism.

5.3 Behaviourism and intentionality

Although behaviourism is unpromising as an account of the nature of sensations and conscious experience generally, and therefore as an approach to a *general* solution to the mind–body problem, it looks promising as the basis for dealing with one large component of that problem: intentionality. Let us look more closely at this suggestion.

If holistic behaviourism is the right approach, then having thoughts with content, or thoughts about things, is just having certain kinds of behavioural dispositions. But that doesn't take us far. What kinds of dispositions matter? If we can't link each thought with its own special disposition, what use is this approach? Those are understandable reactions. However, although it would have been nice if we could have correlated individual thoughts with individual dispositions, the fact that holistic behaviourism fails to do that doesn't prevent it from throwing light on our problems. Holistic behaviourism's big idea can be broken into two components. The first is this: that there is no more involved in having thoughts about things, or contentful thoughts generally, than having the right sorts of behavioural dispositions. The second is that there is no more involved in the fact that *thoughts* are about things than there is in *behaviour* being about things. I have said enough for the present about the first component; the second needs some explanation.

5.4 Aboutness and behaviour

Consider a blackbird on the lawn, first listening, then pecking, then suddenly dragging a worm out and eating it. The mere act of listening can't be said to be "about" the worm which the bird eventually eats, since presumably it has not yet latched on to that particular prey. But when it pulls the worm from the ground, then swallows it piece by piece, there is a sense in which its behaviour can be said to be about the worm. This is not just a matter of the behaviour being *caused* by the worm. One object can have effects on another without the first's behaviour being about the second's. In order for something to be a candidate for behaving in ways that can sensibly be described as "about" something, it must be an organism or system with certain sorts of capacities. The blackbird distinguishes itself from sticks and stones by showing patterns of behaviour of kinds that encourage us to describe it as having some intelligence, as perceiving things around it, as some sort of agent. Just what conditions have to be satisfied by something in order for it to count as capable of behaviour indicating aboutness is not clear: I will return to that question later (Ch. 7). Meanwhile, the blackbird can continue to serve as an example.

The blackbird's behaviour can sensibly be described as being about or directed at the worm. Not only that: it is also an example of the kind of behaviour that enables us to acquire and use the idea of aboutness, so that it can help us to grasp what it is for behaviour to be about something. We can if we like back up the broad claim that the blackbird's behaviour is *about the worm* with more detailed descriptions. For example, the bird keeps looking at the worm, keeps pulling until it is out of the ground, aims its beak at it, bites pieces out of it, swallows these pieces – and so on. The bird's behaviour also seems likely to satisfy various relevant counterfactual conditions: if the worm were moved away a little, the bird would follow it; if the bird accidentally picked up a non-worm it would spit it out and go back to the worm; and so on. Such things both make it intelligible to say that the bird's behaviour is about or directed at the worm, and help to explain what it means to say such a thing.

Can we say that the bird also has beliefs or desires about the worm? Or intentions with respect to it? Does it have *thoughts* about it? Here we probably need more details about both the bird and its situation. How intelligent is it really? How much of its behaviour consists of mere reflexes which, when activated in sequence, cause behaviour that looks intelligent but isn't? Some philosophers would argue that to be capable of having beliefs, desires and intentions in the full sense of those words requires language. But we need not pursue that debate here, since it is an issue for a whole range of different philosophical approaches to the mind, not just for behaviourism. Some behaviourists too will insist that language is necessary for genuine belief, desire, intention and thought; others will point to the impressive cognitive achievements of some languageless creatures, and maintain that non-linguistic behaviour can have sufficient complexity to warrant the ascription of intentional states to them (see Ch. 7).

Regardless of whether language is necessary for genuine intentional states, behaviourists will insist that using language is just another type of behaviour. Certainly it enables creatures to coordinate their behaviour in new and highly complicated ways, and generally to move up to higher levels of cognitive sophistication than languageless creatures are capable of. Certainly also (at least this is plausible), if a creature *does* have a language, then its normal language-using behaviour manifests beliefs, desires, intentions and other sorts of intentional states. But using spoken or written words is none the less just a way of behaving.

The behaviourist can say that when a language-user speaks or writes, these activities, together with the fact that behind them lies a complex network of nested behavioural dispositions, constitute expressions of thoughts, beliefs, desires, intentions, hopes and so on. But the behaviourist will insist that such "expressions of thoughts" and the rest do not require *further* parallel sequences of events lying behind them. It is a mistake, according to behaviourism, to assume that there are such things (see, for example, Wittgenstein 1953: §§318, 329. Ryle wrote that "When I do something intelligently, i.e. thinking what I am doing, I am doing one thing and not two. My performance has a special procedure and manner, not special antecedents": 1949: 32). Behaviourists are of course ready to concede that, as Ryle emphasized, "Keeping our thoughts to ourselves is a sophisticated accomplishment" (*ibid.*: 27). But what they are getting at is not that we don't say things "in our heads". It is that thinking is not something over and above actual behaviour, whether overt or covert.

The behaviourist can also say that as an individual engages in the process of acquiring the hugely complex system of interlocking behavioural dispositions that constitutes possession of a language, "aboutness" becomes correspondingly more complicated. The way the blackbird's behaviour is about the worm is relatively uncomplicated. The way a physicist's talk of atoms is about atoms depends on having acquired whole complexes of skills and dispositions that constitute an understanding of physical theory. No one can even see an atom, much less peck at it.

5.5 Aboutness, reference and content

There is a temptation to assume that *aboutness* must be a single, unitary relation; similarly to assume there is some single, unitary relation between thoughts and the world that constitutes the former having their particular *contents*; also to assume there is a unitary relation of *reference* between words and things. Behaviourism offers an alternative approach.

What is common to the way the blackbird's pecking is about the worm, and the way the physicist's use of sentences including the word "atom" is about atoms? Behaviourists are under no pressure to suggest an answer. It is our use of the word "about" and related expressions that determines our readiness to use it in these and countless other cases; but there is no reason to assume that for that reason there must be a single relation which unites them – other than the trivial fact that the same word strikes us as appropriate. Our genetic make-up and culture are such that when we are brought up in an English-speaking community we find it natural to agree with one another in the ways we use words; and the fact that we do so enables our verbal behaviour to do its useful work for us. We just pick up the right patterns of behaviour and the right complexes of associated dispositions; and all that is needed for us to be able to coordinate our behaviour with other people is that our verbal *behaviour* exhibits a sufficient degree of conformity. Behaviourism has no need to look for anything beyond. In particular it has no need to seek a unitary relation of aboutness.

Those remarks apply just as well to the special kind of aboutness known as reference. The name "Aristotle" refers to that man, Aristotle. The name "Paris" refers to that city. The word "two" refers to the number 2. "Potatoes" refers to potatoes. And so on. Behaviourists don't have to maintain that all cases of reference share something in common. And just as pecking can be a way of dealing with a worm, so using a referring expression (normally in a sentence) can be a way of dealing with its referent. Saying "Send Lucy my love" is a way of making something happen to Lucy. Saying "Potatoes, please" is a way of making something happen to some potatoes so that they land on my plate – just as going into the garden and digging is a way of (eventually) achieving the same result. To most behaviourists it seems misguided to expect there to be a *single* relation that connects referring expressions with their referents. The ways in which our abilities and dispositions to use linguistic expressions are linked with the various sorts of things we say they refer to seem too diverse, and in detail too particular, for that project to make sense.

Very much the same goes for the *contents* of our beliefs, desires, intentions and other intentional states, and of our verbal utterances. Why should their being contentful require the existence of a single (non-trivial) relation? The patterns of behaviour by means of which we are able to say what we believe, desire, intend and the rest

– the patterns of behaviour that constitute the utterance of contentful sentences – are each connected in multifarious ways with other patterns of behaviour, and these in turn with things in the world. These connections account for the fact that our utterances have the contents they do. Behaviourists can therefore say that they have sufficient explanation of contentfulness in general to remove the apparent mystery of how thoughts relate to the world. What compels them to say more?

5.6 Two behaviour-based projects: Davidson and Dennett

You may object that it's not good enough to offer a broad-brush general explanation of the aboutness and contentfulness of intentional states. What we need, you may think, is a systematic account that will enable us to fix, for any arbitrary intentional state, what constitutes its having whatever content it does have. One behaviour-based project of that sort is Davidson's. This is his project of "radical interpretation".

Suppose we find ourselves in a community that is completely strange to us. We don't know their language and are not familiar with their culture. We have no bilingual guides, no grammars, no dictionaries. We aim to interpret their utterances, to understand what they mean, and to discover their beliefs and other intentional states. How are we to set about it? There is a serious problem with this project of "radical interpretation". If we already knew what the foreigners meant by their utterances we could use that to discover their beliefs and desires. If we knew what they believed and desired we could use that to discover what they meant. Since in the situation imagined we know neither, "in interpreting utterances from scratch – in *radical* interpretation – we must somehow deliver simultaneously a theory of belief and a theory of meaning" (Davidson 1974: 144).

A key component of Davidson's approach is the assumption that we must find a suitable "theory of truth" for the community's language. This theory, on the lines proposed by Tarski, will have syntactic rules which fix the grammatical sentences of the language, and semantic rules which give the meanings of those sentences via links between the predicates and other expressions of the language on the one hand, and things and features of the world on the other.

Famously Tarski imposed a certain necessary condition on such a theory of truth. It must entail all sentences of the same form as:

"Snow is white" is true in L if and only if snow is white.

These are the "T-sentences". Tarski aimed to explain the concept of truth without using either it or such associated semantic concepts as that of reference. Davidson in contrast assumes we already have a reasonably good grasp of the concept of truth and aims to use a Tarskian truth theory to provide an understanding of the meanings of sentences. Provided the theory of truth is constrained by sufficiently strong conditions, Davidson thinks, the T-sentences will serve actually to give the meanings of the sentences of the language. It would take us too far out of our way to pursue the debates on this project here. But it is an excellent example – indeed pretty well the only one – of an approach entirely compatible with behaviourism, which goes beyond broad-brush statements to tackle the details of how behaviour could be interpreted.

A different approach to the nature of intentionality, also consistent with behaviourism, has been developed by Dennett. His approach started off as a version of *instrumentalism*, according to which the intentional vocabulary of believing, desiring, intending and the rest is strictly a convenient device for describing, explaining and predicting behaviour, without claiming that its key terms pick out features of reality. In his classic paper "Intentional Systems" (1971) he distinguishes three "stances" we might adopt to explaining and predicting the behaviour of a system.

We adopt the *physical stance* when for example the computer's hardware fails and we call in the engineer. "Why does pressing the 'A' key have no effect?" – "Because the wire supposed to connect it to the rest of the machinery is broken." This stance involves treating the machine as just a physical system whose behaviour is to be explained in purely physical terms, backed up by physical laws. Of course there are different levels at which such physical explanations may be appropriate. Dennett points out that because of the complexity of low-level explanations, "the physical stance is generally reserved for instances of breakdown" (1971: 5).

When a mechanical object is working normally we generally adopt the *design stance*, and make our predictions "solely from knowledge or assumptions about the system's functional design, irrespective of the physical constitution or condition of the innards of the particular object" (1971: 4). "Press the button marked 'redial' and it will dial the last number again", for example.

But many systems are too complex for their behaviour to be readily explicable or predictable even from the design stance. A favourite example of Dennett's is the chess-playing computer. Even if we knew this machine's program we couldn't refer to its program to explain the details of its actual behaviour. Instead we assume we can treat it as if it knows how to play chess, aims to win, and is rational (if only in the restricted field of chess). When playing against it we ascribe beliefs and desires to it on that basis; and this policy works. With experience of its play we can among other things come to ascribe to it such general beliefs as that "It thinks it's a good idea to get its Queen out early". This policy is the *intentional stance.*

In a later presentation of his views Dennett encapsulates the idea of the intentional stance as follows:

> First you decide to treat the object whose behaviour is to be predicted as a rational agent; then you figure out what beliefs that agent ought to have, given its place in the world and its purpose. Then you figure out what desires it ought to have, on the same considerations, and finally you predict that this rational agent will act to further its goals in the light of its beliefs. (1987: 17)

He holds, among other things, that anything:

> whose behaviour is well predicted by this strategy [the "intentional strategy"] is in the fullest sense of the word a believer. *What it is* to be a true believer is to be an *intentional system,* a system whose behaviour is reliably and voluminously predictable via the intentional strategy. (1987: 15)

This approach implies that to enquire whether something which satisfies the conditions for being an intentional system *really* has the beliefs and desires we find it so useful to ascribe to it is to miss the point. If Dennett is right there is no room for something to satisfy those conditions and fail "really" to have beliefs and desires.

Originally the intentional strategy was strictly a means to the end of being able to make useful predictions and supply a special kind of explanation – belief–desire explanation. It was not also regarded as a way to discover some further-back realities constituting the system's real beliefs and desires. In later writings Dennett rejects the ascription to him of the description "instrumentalist" and insists that "belief is a perfectly objective phenomenon" (1987: 15).

We have noticed the main features of behaviourism, and briefly noted two important and interesting developments that are thoroughly consistent with it. It is now time to consider some difficulties other than the familiar one of sensations.

5.7 Galen Strawson's Weather Watchers

In his book *Mental Reality* (1994) Galen Strawson challenges a fundamental assumption made by many contemporary psychologists and philosophers of mind. This assumption is that:

> mental life is linked to behaviour in such a way that reference to behaviour, or at least to dispositions to behaviour, enters essentially – constitutively and centrally – into any adequate account of the fundamental nature of almost all, if not all, mental states and occurrences, like emotions, sensations, thoughts, beliefs, and desires.   (1994: 29)

Strawson calls this assumption *neo-behaviourism*, since although it is obviously akin to behaviourism as discussed in this chapter, it is not identical with it because it leaves room for the nature of the internal processing to matter. (He says behaviourism "has gone out of fashion because it is plainly false" (1994: 31).) His main assault on neo-behaviourism consists of the description of what he regards as a counter-example: the Weather Watchers. If he is right, then he will have refuted more than behaviourism.

The Weather Watchers are rooted to the ground and "profoundly interested in the local weather". They have "sensations, thoughts, emotions, beliefs, desires" but they produce no sort of (overt) behaviour and are constitutionally incapable of it. "They are not even disposed to behave in any way" (1994: 251). Strawson notes that there can be purely mental action, like doing mental arithmetic.

However, although he could have described the Weather Watchers as capable of performing and intending to perform mental actions, he prefers to concentrate on a version of his story according to which they cannot act and are not disposed to act in any way, and do not have intentions. In spite of all that, they have "many *mental-activity* dispositions: emotional-reaction dispositions, desire-formation dispositions, train-of-thought dispositions, automatic sensory-experience-interpretation dispositions", which are "just like dispositions we possess ourselves" (1994: 258). Thus he provides a kind of basis for them to have a mental life. It's just that this mental life is severed from any connection with overt behaviour.

Strawson claims it follows from his description that "we never have any good reason to attribute mental states to" the Weather Watchers, and "nothing that even gives us any prima facie reason to suppose that they do" (1994: 254, 257). Although that would be true if behaviourism were correct, I don't think it is true in fact. It overlooks the possibility that we might be able to discover enough about how the Weather Watchers' innards work to conclude that they have mental states. (He notes the possibility that "highly complicated nervous-system-like activity might weigh with us" (1994: 257) but that is not what I have in mind.) Of course, in order to be in a position to use evidence about their innards we should need to have a good non-neo-behaviouristic account of what it takes to have mental states; and it is not clear that such an account is available. But I don't think Strawson says anything which rules out the possibility I have mentioned.

Is the example coherent? Some philosophers will object that if there is no publicly available evidence that the Weather Watchers have mental states, then it makes no sense to say they have them. Strawson (rightly, in my opinion) leaves aside that objection, which rests on dubious assumptions. He does discuss a number of other objections, notably that "it isn't really intelligible to attribute desires (and beliefs) to a creature that lacks any disposition to action or behaviour" (1994: 264). The core of his reply is this: "the fundamental and only essential element in desire is *just:* wanting (or liking) something" (1994: 266); and although this no doubt entails being disposed to be satisfied or pleased if one gets what one wants, it doesn't also necessarily require one to want to do something about getting it. (You might wonder whether it enables him to distinguish wanting from hoping, though.) He points out that consideration of the situation of languageless creatures and babies may help to make this clear, and:

> Whether it does or not, there is no contradiction in the idea that even a creature capable of conscious thought with languagelike structure might want something while lacking any conception of the possibility of being able to do anything about getting it. (1994: 266)

If Strawson's example of the Weather Watchers, together with his supplementary reasoning, do indeed refute neo-behaviourism, then dispositions to overt behaviour are not *necessary* for having mental states. However, behaviouristically inclined philosophers might still urge that they are *sufficient*. In the following two sections we shall consider some arguments to the contrary.

5.8 The pantomime horse

The pantomime horse, as it ambles about the stage, behaves a bit more intelligently than an ordinary horse. For one thing it understands English. For another, it seems to grasp the situation of the human actors. It anticipates their actions and makes life hard for them, apparently on purpose. But we know it isn't really an intelligent creature. There is only a horse costume with two people inside it. None the less this thing behaves intelligently, and is also disposed to behave intelligently, thanks to the settled policy of its operators, Front Legs and Back Legs. If behaviourism is correct, then the right behaviour and dispositions are both necessary and sufficient for having mental states. Since the pantomime horse has the right behaviour and dispositions but doesn't have mental states, it is a counter-example. How could behaviourists reply?

They might challenge the assumption that the pantomime horse has the right dispositions. If somebody bursts on to the stage and announces that Front Legs's house is on fire you won't get horse-like behaviour, or even pantomime-horse-like behaviour; you'll get collapse and split-up. However, break-up of the system hardly counts as part of its behaviour, so that objection is unconvincing. As far as the pantomime horse's actual behaviour is concerned, we can suppose that the two operators are fanatically determined to ensure that not only *does* it behave appropriately, but that it is *disposed* to behave appropriately.

Behaviourists might now reply that in that case the pantomime horse really does have mental states. That seems odd, but then lots of odd things turn out to be true. However, what makes this example seem "counter" need not be mere uninstructed pretheoretic intuitions. Consider how the pantomime horse's behaviour is caused. It is caused by Front Legs's and Back Legs's decisions, not by the decisions of any autonomous intelligent being. The situation is like that of a glove puppet. Small children easily think of a glove puppet as an autonomous being which makes its own decisions, understands English and is generally intelligent. But because we know what is going on, we know there is really no such intelligent autonomous being. There is only something made to produce the *illusion* of being an independent intelligent creature. The pantomime horse is a puppet whose only difference from a glove puppet is that the puppeteers are inside its "skin". If we regard Front Legs, Back Legs and the horse "skin" as together forming a single system, then that system has the right behavioural dispositions for an intelligent being. But because all the intelligence, all the decision-making, all the causation of behaviour, is the responsibility of the two operators, there is no candidate to occupy the role of an autonomous intelligent system apart from them. And if the pantomime horse *is* to be an intelligent system, it must be one that is different from either or both of its two operators.

We can imagine analogous but more complex systems, for example an artificial giant, superficially like a man – like Gulliver in Lilliput perhaps – but controlled by the people inside it much as the pantomime horse's behaviour is controlled by its operators. (See Kirk 1994: 117–23.) To end this chapter I will discuss a thought-provoking example devised by Ned Block.

5.9 Block's machines

Block's main argument against behaviourism starts from considering the famous "Turing Test". Turing considered that the question "Can machines think?" was too unclear to be properly discussed, and suggested it should be replaced by questions based on the

"Imitation Game". The key idea is that an interrogator questions in turn a human being and a computer, each for the same fixed period of time. The questions are to be communicated purely in writing, for example via a computer keyboard and screen. The interrogator's job is to try to discover, within that fixed time interval, which is the computer. Turing believed that "in about fifty years' time" (which would have meant about 2000):

> it will be possible to program computers . . . to make them play the imitation game so well that an average interrogator will not have more than 70 per cent chance of making the right identification after five minutes of questioning. (1950: 57)

Simplified, the "Turing Test" of intelligence – it has to be confined to purely "conversational" intelligence – is simply to discover whether the system being tested in this way can make the interrogator think it is a human being. For various reasons Block suggests a modified conception of intelligence: the *Neo-Turing conception*, according to which intelligence is a matter of having the right capacities. Since Block is attacking behaviourism, he opposes this idea. But he reasonably thinks it is a good way of putting the behaviourists' position. According to this conception, then, "Intelligence (or, more accurately, conversational intelligence) is the capacity to produce a sensible sequence of verbal responses to a sequence of verbal stimuli, whatever they may be" (Block 1981: 18). The word "sensible" here may strike you as question-begging: doesn't being sensible entail being intelligent? But remember that Block is not defending the Neo-Turing conception of conversational intelligence: here he is just trying to state his opponents' position as fairly as possible: he's bending over backwards to accommodate them. Block goes on to describe a way of programming a computer that will on the one hand ensure that the machine has the capacities required for meeting the Turing conception of conversational intelligence, but on the other hand clearly fails to endow the machine with intelligence.

First we fix the time limit for the test, say (following Turing) five minutes. Then we establish the maximum number of characters typable in that period on an ordinary keyboard of, say, 60 characters. Pretend the maximum is 1,000 characters. Now consider the set of *all* sequences of up to 1,000 characters (this will be 60^{1000} on our assumptions – a monstrous number). A simple program will enable all these sequences to be ground out, rubbish and all. (It's diverting, though not really relevant, to think of what will be included in these sequences. They will include all true histories of the universe capable of being expressed in 1,000 characters; all true biographies of everyone who will ever have lived, assuming only a finite number of people; an accurate account of your own life up to the present moment; an accurate account of the rest of your life; a detailed account of what you did over the last ten minutes – together, of course, with all *false* stories of these and all other possible kinds. Nor are these sequences confined to what can be expressed in English: they will include whatever can be set down by means of the standard keyboard. But chiefly the sequences will be more or less pure rubbish.)

Having churned out these zillions of sequences, we assign millions of research students to sort them out. What they have to do is discard all sequences that fail to meet the following condition: they can be regarded as *conversations between two people in which the second participant's contributions are sensible in the context of the whole conversation up to that point*. We then put all these "possible five-minute conversations" into the computer's memory, marking off the segments supposedly contributed by each of the two participants. Finally we can program the computer as follows. When some characters are typed in, it is to search the stored possible conversations for the alphanumerically first one whose initial segment matches what has been typed in so far. Having found it, it is to put out the next segment of that same possible conversation. And so on.

It doesn't matter what the interrogator types in. It can perfectly well be total rubbish, since all that matters is that the *second* participant's contributions make sense in the context of the whole conversation. Nor does everything intelligible have to be in English, although we would do well to instruct the research students to make the replies consistent with a fairly definite character on the part of the supposed respondent (the computer); so it wouldn't be a good idea to make it appear to know too many foreign languages. On the other hand there's nothing to stop it being capable of showing it can learn to use foreign expressions.

Now, although this program is extremely simple, it clearly endows the system with capacities which guarantee it satisfies the Neo-Turing conception of intelligence. Whatever the tester throws at it, its responses are sensible in the context. Notice especially that the program cannot be represented as a simple look-up table or stimulus–response scheme, by which a given stimulus always causes a fixed response. How the machine responds depends not just on the inputs, but on the stored possible conversations, so it is highly unlikely that the same input will cause the same output within a given five-minute test. (It is irrelevant if it repeats its performance in *successive* tests, since the Neo-Turing conception concerns what it would do for a single five-minute period.)

Some people get cross about the completely impracticable scale of the operation. The appropriate reply, it seems to me, is that we are concerned purely with a theory about what intelligence involves, so that it doesn't matter whether the counter-example is not workable in practice so long as it's theoretically sound.

Nor, I suggest, are objections based on the machine's ignorance of what is going on around it to the point. All that is being tested is its intelligence. On that basis it can well be treated as lacking any sources of information other than the interrogator's keyboard.

In spite of the fact that a computer so programmed satisfies the Neo-Turing conception of conversational intelligence, Block argues that we know enough about it to be sure it has "the intelligence of a toaster" (1981: 21). He remarks that "all the intelligence it exhibits is that of its programmers"; but that, though true, is misleading, since it could theoretically have come into existence by a cosmic freak, as a result of an electric storm in the computer centre (as he points out in a footnote).

Behaviourists may still grit their teeth and insist that the thing really is intelligent. However, this insistence is powerfully opposed by an assumption which in my experience almost everyone concedes. Almost everyone I have asked agrees that we can't count a system as intelligent unless it is capable of working out its own way of reacting to whatever situation it finds itself in. I take this to be solid evidence for what we can call the *moderate realism of folk psychology*. Folk psychology doesn't seem to be purely behaviouristic. It seems to impose a few rough and ready constraints on anything that it is going to count as an intelligent or conscious system. For present purposes the relevant constraint seems to be that genuine intelligence requires the system in question to be capable of working out its own behaviour on the basis of its own assessment of its situation. This realism is only moderate, however. It requires only that there be *some* processes going on that can constitute the system's cobbling together its own decisions about how to behave. Folk psychology doesn't seem to provide any basis for claims much stronger than that.

If that is correct, it is enough by itself to show that the Block machine is not intelligent. In no sense can it be said to work out its own behaviour, since everything it does is determined by its store of possible conversations. Nor can it be said to understand what it is saying, since it would put out rubbish just as promptly as intelligent remarks. It's not as if, like a genuinely intelligent subject, it were capable of any sort of analysis, whether syntactic or semantic, of either the inputs typed in by the interrogator or what it puts out itself.

Block goes on to explain how these ideas can be extended to apply to all kinds of behaviour, not just verbal. Corresponding to possible ten-minute conversations are possible total life histories of *x* years. On assumptions that are not unreasonable, the resulting robot will have behavioural capacities which ensure that it produces sensible behaviour in whatever possible situation it finds itself, from birth to the end of *x* years.

5.10 Conclusion

We started by noting that behaviourism encounters serious problems in connection with sensations and other conscious experiences, but seems more promising when it comes to beliefs, desires, intentions and so on. The extreme reductionist variety – requiring logical equivalence between psychological statements and statements about behaviour and dispositions – is unlikely to work even for intentional states. However, at first sight the global variety still seemed capable of explaining them; further investigation showed ways in which this might be done. We also noted that Davidson's suggestions for carrying out the project of radical interpretation are consistent with this sort of behaviourism, as is Dennett's "intentional systems" approach.

Galen Strawson's Weather Watchers raise difficulties, however, and have the important implication that behavioural dispositions are not necessary for being a subject of mental states. Things like the pantomime horse and Block's machines imply that even the right sorts of behavioural dispositions are not sufficient for it either.

Behaviourism continues to offer valuable insights into the relations between mental states and behaviour, yet still appears to fall short of supplying a really satisfactory approach to mind–body problems. In Chapter 6 we shall consider whether functionalism does a better job.

Main points in Chapter 5

1. There are significantly different varieties of (philosophical) behaviourism. The "holistic" or "global" kind does not require the production of behaviouristic equivalents for sentences describing individual mental states (§§5.1, 5.2, 5.3).

2. Although behaviourism is unconvincing as an approach to sensations (5.1) it offers a promising approach to explaining intentionality, including "aboutness" and "reference" (§§5.4, 5.5).

3. These notions may well not be unitary (§5.5).

4. Davidson has worked out a systematic approach to explaining the meanings of sentences, also the contents of individual beliefs and other intentional states, exploiting Tarski-type truth theories in a way consistent with behaviourism (§5.6).

5. Dennett distinguishes three possible "stances" that we may take when attempting to explain the behaviour of a system. As originally presented, the "intentional" stance is purely instrumental (§5.6).

6. Galen Strawson attacks what he calls "neo-behaviourism" – which is broader than behaviourism itself – using the example of the "Weather Watchers" (§5.7).

7. In spite of philosophical behaviourism's valuable insights, it is vulnerable to counter-examples which appear to demolish its claim that the nature of the internal processing in a behaving system doesn't matter from the point of view of what its mental states are (§§5.8, 5.9).

Further reading
Both Ryle (1949) and Wittgenstein (1953) promoted a behaviour-based approach to most mental states, although neither seems to have been fully a behaviourist in the sense discussed here.

There is sympathetic criticism of behaviourism in Armstrong (1968: ch. 5). Block (1981) includes other objections to behaviourism than the one based on the machine discussed in the text. Smith & Jones (1986: 144–51) usefully distinguish between "hard" behaviourism, which attempts to use mere bodily movements as the outputs, and "soft" behaviourism, which uses everyday action-based concepts.

Davidson's project is developed in a number of papers in his 1984 collection, and discussed in many essays in LePore (ed.) (1986).

Dennett's first version of his conception of the intentional stance is in Dennett (1971). For its later forms see Dennett (1987: esp. 13–42).

6 Functionalism

Philosophers working on the psycho-physical identity thesis around the middle of the last century were focusing chiefly on consciousness rather than intentionality. As far as beliefs, desires and other intentional states were concerned, they tended to think a behaviouristic account was possible. However, we have seen that merely asserting that conscious experiences are identical with brain processes is not enough. Even if the identities hold, what is it about brain processes that enables them to provide for conscious experience? Somehow it must be made intelligible that things like the activation of neurones should constitute sensations and experiences. When philosophers started looking for ways of dealing with this difficulty, some of their proposals turned out to apply not just to experiences but to the rest of mental life too. They were in fact varieties of *functionalism*. Although many philosophers favour this approach, it has its critics. John Searle has remarked, "If you are tempted to functionalism, I believe you do not need refutation, you need help" (1992: 9).

6.1 Leading up to functionalism

Consider this statement:

> Different mental states tend to be caused by different sorts of external things, and in turn to cause different sorts of behaviour.

It is at least hard to dispute. It doesn't say that mental states *are* just behaviour, or even just behavioural dispositions. It says something that even Descartes would accept. Such reflections led to the idea that a mental state's causal relationships were *characteristic* of it: that each mental state was distinguished by its own unique pattern of causal links with sensory stimulation, with behavioural consequences, and with other mental states.

At first this was regarded as no more than a way to back up the identity thesis:

Question: "What entitles us to say that mental state M is identical with brain state B?"

Answer: "We know by observation and reflection that mental state M is caused in such and such ways, and has such and such effects. We also know that brain state B is caused in the same ways and has the same effects. Knowing that M and B share the same pattern of causal relations justifies the claim that M is in fact identical with B."

6.2 A crucial step

Then some philosophers came to think that the causal/theoretical relationships in question provided more than justification; more even than a way to pick out just which brain processes were involved in particular types of mental state. The new thought was that these causal or theoretical relationships specified the actual *nature* of mental states. On this view, having mental states is having states that stand in the right sorts of causal relations to sensory inputs, behavioural outputs and other mental states. That is the commonest variety of functionalism.

Here are some possible illustrations of the idea: (i) What makes a particular internal state of mine the belief that it's raining is that it tends to be caused by such facts as that when I look outside I actually see rain; and that it tends to make me think of taking an umbrella if I decide to go out. (ii) What makes my internal state a desire for a cup of coffee is (among many other things) that it tends to be caused by certain bodily changes (to do with when I last had something to drink, for example) and tends to cause me actually to go about making sure I get a cup of coffee. (iii) What makes my internal state a belief that the battle of Hastings was fought in 1066 is that it was caused by complicated verbal and pictorial inputs in my childhood, themselves caused by remoter events which, indirectly, were actually caused by the battle in question; and tends to cause me to do things like answer "1066" when I am asked for the date of the battle of Hastings.

6.3 Some implications

In spite of its origins in attempts to justify the psycho-physical identity thesis, functionalism leaves the identity thesis behind. If functionalism is correct, physicalists have no need to concern themselves with statements of identity. If it is correct, then in order to show that physicalism is true it will be enough to show that the relevant causal/functional relations hold in a purely physical system. Of course it is not trivial to show that functionalism *is* correct: far from it. But at least the problems of the identity thesis are avoided.

Recalling behaviourism's weakness over sensations, let us focus on the case of pain. According to functionalism, being in pain is not just a matter of behavioural dispositions, but a kind of internal state. If you enquire what *kind* of internal state, the answer is: *whatever* internal state does the right job or performs the right functions. The following might be a functionalist first stab at a definition of what it is to be in pain:

(D)   *x* is in pain if and only if *x* is in a state typically caused by damage to *x*'s body and typically causing *x* to wince, groan, or scream, depending on the amount of damage.

No doubt (D) is too simple; but it gives a good idea of one kind of functionalist approach to our problems. Pretend that (D) is a correct definition, and further that the firing of C-fibres fits that definition. On those assumptions the occurrence of C-fibre firings in *x entails* that *x* is in pain. In terms explained towards the end of Chapter 3, pain *logically supervenes* on C-fibre firings; and if the narrowly physical truths about a person include that their C-fibres are firing at a time *t*, then those truths *strictly imply* that the person is in pain at *t*. In this way functionalism promises to explain how it is that physicalism is true, thereby solving the mind–body problem.

And it does so without falling foul of the multiple realizability objection, since although satisfaction of (D) by C-fibre firing entails that the person is in pain, (D) does not also imply that anyone in pain must have their C-fibres firing. (D) is entirely compatible with there being indefinitely many different ways in which pain might be instantiated or realized.

Relatedly, functionalism in general offers an approach to understanding the nature of mental states according to which *the materials from which a subject of mental states is constructed are irrelevant* provided they have the necessary "functional organization". This is fundamentally important. Think of a watch. What makes it a watch? Must it be made of steel? Obviously not. Must it have hands? No: there are digital watches. Must it have a spring? Again no. All that is necessary is that it have a functional organization which ensures that it does *something* that marks the time in a convenient way. Similarly, functionalists maintain, in order for something to have mental states, all that is necessary is the right kind of functional organization. In order for one of its states to be this particular mental state, it need only have the right causal role in that organization. It doesn't matter what the system is made of or how it is constructed. Hilary Putnam put it vividly: "we could be made of Swiss cheese and it wouldn't matter" (1975c: 291. I don't think he meant it would actually be feasible to make a brain out of cheese).

That functionalism has this implication is illustrated by (D), which leaves it entirely open what sort of processes could satisfy the *definiens*. Indeed, (D) doesn't even require those processes to be physical: if there were non-physical processes capable of doing the necessary job, then dualistic systems could be subjects of mental states just as well as physical systems. So although functionalism is an extremely useful approach for physicalists – all the functionalists I know of are physicalists – strictly it is neutral between physicalism and dualism. However, if functionalism is correct, we don't seem to have any reason to suppose that human thought and feeling involve anything beyond the physical.

6.4 Scope for variations

There is plenty of scope for differences under the broad banner of functionalism, for example over how to specify inputs and outputs.

I have been using neutral terms like "internal states", "sensory inputs" and "behavioural outputs". As specific examples of inputs I have used a range of items such as *seeing rain* (in connection with the analysis of the belief that it is raining); *bodily damage* (in the case of pain); *receiving verbal reports* (date of the battle of Hastings). As examples of outputs I have used *making sure I get a cup of coffee*; *answering "1066"*; *wincing, groaning, screaming*. Examples of internal states have been *thinking of taking an umbrella*; *pain (itself)*. These items belong to different categories, but I have tended to specify them in terms of everyday psychological expressions. One reason for being dissatisfied with this choice is that it seems to introduce circularity. The functionalist project is to explain psychological states in terms of functional organisation and causal relations. If inputs or outputs cannot be described except in everyday psychological terms, the project seems to be stuck.

One way out is to attempt to specify inputs and outputs in purely physical or at any rate neutral terms: terms which do not involve everyday psychological concepts. For several reasons that is extremely difficult, if not impossible. In any case it would only strike one as necessary if the aim were not only to produce functional-term logical equivalents for psychological descriptions, but to do so in such a way that psychological descriptions could actually be done away with. That strongly reductionist project is not what most functionalists are about. (For discussion see Smith & Jones 1986: 171–3).

A different approach was suggested by David Lewis. He exploited two basic ideas. One was that the best way to identify types of mental states was indeed via ordinary everyday psychology, regarded as a loose kind of theory. Now, mental states are taken to be unobservable. To deal with this fact Lewis exploited another idea: Frank Ramsey's proposal that those special predicates of a given theory which refer to *unobservable* items could be defined on the basis of the theory as a whole, including of course its laws. The complete set of terms belonging to the theory includes not only its special terms – the expressions referring to those unobservable items themselves – but others as well, including mathematical terms, terms referring to observables, and any others that may be assumed to be understood in advance of being introduced via the theory. Then the idea is to treat the theory's special terms as *variables*, say "X", "Y" and "Z", and prefix the theory with existential quantifiers to the effect that "There exist X, Y and Z such that . . .". What replaces the dots is a statement of the theory itself. A sentence of that form is the "Ramsey sentence" for the theory. It says that *there are* items standing to each other in the complex network of relationships specified by the theory as a whole.

Lewis argues that the Ramsey sentence for a theory T *gives meaning* to the special terms of T by being an "implicit functional definition" (Lewis 1972: 251). T specifies the functional or causal roles occupied by the referents of the special terms. He goes on to suggest that we should "Think of common-sense psychology as a term-introducing scientific theory", and collect all the platitudes we can think of "regarding the causal relations of mental states, sensory stimuli, and motor responses", and add to them "all the platitudes to the effect that one mental state falls under another – 'toothache is a kind of pain', and the like". We should include "only platitudes which are common knowledge among us: everyone knows them, everyone knows that everyone else knows them, and so on" (1972: 256). If that suggestion can be made to work, then each type of mental state is *definable* on the basis of its place in the complex network of states, types of input and types of behavioural output. The "theory" consisting of the relevant "platitudes" "defines the mental states by reference to their causal relations to stimuli, responses, and each other" (1972: 256).

Is it legitimate to use the platitudes of common-sense psychology to get started? There is a question over what to include among them. Should we include *all* our everyday psychological beliefs? That seems risky, since some of them may well be mistaken, in which case the Ramsey sentences will be false. If on the other hand we restrict the commonplaces to ones that seem reasonably solid, we risk failing to determine which predicate applies to which state. In his article Lewis suggests moves which lessen the force of this objection.

Another difficulty is that it seems that the platitudes which are "common knowledge among us" could easily leave out many highly relevant truths. These would not only be items of scientific knowledge. They would include whatever truths may emerge from philosophical reflection on the nature of consciousness, perception and cognition generally. Perhaps that complaint could be remedied by allowing the "theory" to include not only what is common knowledge, but also whatever is implied by it.

One suggestion for dealing with such difficulties yields another variety of functionalism. It is to use *scientific* psychology, not everyday psychology, as the theoretical basis. But apart from the fact that there is considerable rivalry among the various approaches to scientific psychology, none seems to have produced a completed theory. That doesn't mean the project must be abandoned; but it does mean we have to be more patient than philosophers often are. Notice, however, that while Lewis's approach promises actually to explain the *meanings* of terms for mental states – these meanings are defined by the functional roles specified by the whole theory – the science-based approach could not claim to do the same. It is an open question how far, if at all, a future scientific psychology would use expressions that could be rendered in terms of everyday psychology.

Although it is an appealing idea to *define* mental states in terms of their causal roles, functionalists are not compelled to undertake that project. Of course they may push for some strong variety of reductionist physicalism which requires such definitions. But physicalists do not seem forced to be reductionists in any non-trivial sense (§§3.8–3.12). They could abandon the project of defining each type of mental state and restrict themselves to the claim that there is no more to the existence of mental states than there is to states performing causal roles (or whichever other functions might be chosen: evolutionary functions, for example). This would be a global approach corresponding to the global version of behaviourism noted in §5.2. It would still serve the valuable purpose of explaining the general nature of mental states, and how a purely physical system could be a subject of such states.

6.5 Can there be neutral definitions?

Several of the objections to physicalism discussed earlier have also been brought against functionalism. To take an important example, Nagel regarded his objection to physicalism as including an objection to functionalism. Recall that the core of his objection was that physicalism fails to give satisfactory "accounts" of consciousness because it is committed to objective, viewpoint-neutral concepts, while facts about "what it is like" cannot be stated without using viewpoint-relative concepts (§§4.1, 4.2). He concluded that physicalism and functionalism inevitably leave consciousness out. They cannot account for what he calls the "phenomenological features", or "feel", as some philosophers put it.

We saw that this objection works only against a particularly strong variety of physicalism, according to which giving an account of "feel" would require providing statements in neutral terms which actually *gave the meanings* of statements attributing phenomenological features. Nagel's reasoning does seem to undermine that project. But since physicalism in general has no need to attempt it, his reasoning doesn't amount to an objection to physicalism in general. For the same reason it doesn't amount to an objection to functionalism, since even functional definitions of terms expressing phenomenal consciousness would not have to be construed as giving the meanings of those terms. For example, the *definiens* in (D) does not have to be regarded as an attempt to say what "*x* is in pain" *means*; only as an attempt to set out logically necessary and sufficient conditions for being in pain. (I am not suggesting it succeeds.)

Suppose Nagel is right in claiming that physical or functional accounts of mental-state terms cannot give their meanings. Still, for the reasons we have noted, that leaves it open whether functionalism can give logically necessary and sufficient conditions for, say, *consciousness in general*. If it can do that, then although it may not be able to say what the bat's experiences are like for the bat, it may still be able to explain how it is that the bat *has* conscious experiences. For the same reason, it may be able to explain how it is that the mental facts supervene logically on the purely physical facts. If it can do that as well, then it can explain "feel" perfectly well, in spite of not being able to give meaning-equivalents to statements describing the character of experiences.

6.6 "Absent qualia"

In the same article Nagel mentioned a further objection to functionalism. He said of the subjective character of experience:

> It is not captured by any of the familiar, recently devised reductive analyses of the mental, for all of them are logically

compatible with its absence. It is not analyzable in terms of any explanatory system of functional states, or intentional states, since these could be ascribed to robots or automata that behaved like people though they experienced nothing.

(1974: 166f.)

That is a way of putting the so-called "absent qualia" objection to functionalism – although Nagel did not offer supporting argument in his article. The objection in its starkest form is:

(AQ) It is logically possible that something should have all the functional properties required for consciousness, yet not be conscious.

Since functional accounts of mental states are normally supposed to cover *conscious* mental states too, (AQ) as it stands merely begs the question against functionalism. What is needed is argument. There have been various attempts to support (AQ). One of the best known is Block's homunculus-head, which we considered in connection with Chalmers's defence of the conceivability of zombies (§4.9). It looks as if functionalism entails that the homunculus-head is a subject of mental states, including conscious states; but the claim that it is conscious seems implausible. Appealing to this and related arguments, Block and others urge that functionalism is too "liberal": it lets in too much (Block 1978).

Functionalists can proceed in either of two opposite ways. Either they can claim that the homunculus-head lacks some functionally vital feature; or else they can insist that in spite of contrary intuitions it does have conscious experiences. Neither reply is immediately appealing. The claim that the homunculus-head lacks a vital functional feature is hard to sustain in view of its matching a real human being in all the functions performed in human beings as far down as the input–output functions of individual neurones. So this reply seems committed to there being some relevant functions performed *inside* our neurones without effects on their inputs or outputs.

Perhaps, then, functionalists must grit their teeth and insist that the homunculus-head actually would be a conscious subject. It *seems* logically possible that it should not be conscious; but, functionalists can insist, that is not so. After all, mere intuitions were not decisive for the special case of zombies. Why should they be allowed to be decisive for other cases? Arguably this particular thought experiment is a mere intuition pump: a naked appeal to prejudice.

Functionalists can also point to an important distinction between what we might call "surface" functionalism and other kinds. Surface functionalism is indifferent to the nature of the processing inside a system provided there is the right relation between sensory inputs, behavioural outputs and other states. In this respect it is like behaviourism, although of course it still insists that mental states are real internal states of the system and not mere dispositions. One variety of surface functionalism is "machine functionalism" (see Putnam 1975a); another is Dennett's intentional-system functionalism. Lewis's and Armstrong's varieties of causal functionalism, on the other hand, seem not to be surface varieties but (as we might call them) "deep". Surface functionalism appears to be vulnerable to counter-examples such as the pantomime horse and Block's machines (§§5.8, 5.9). That is a reason for supposing that only "deep" varieties of functionalism have a chance of success.

Deep functionalists can then point out that they do not deny that *some* systems whose behavioural capacities are like those of human beings may still lack qualia. Thus the idea of absent qualia in general is compatible with functionalism, and is to be sharply contrasted with the idea of zombies. Those who insist that a system functionally like a human being may still lack qualia can be told they are appealing to mere intuitions.

6.7 "Transposed qualia" again

In Chapter 4, §4.5 we examined the "transposed qualia" objection to physicalism. As an objection to *functionalism* the alleged possibility can be treated in either of two ways, as for the case of absent qualia. One is to follow Dennett and deny that it is a genuine possibility at all. The other is to adopt "deep" functionalism and maintain that a case of transposed qualia could be underlain by internal functional differences, hence is no problem for functionalism in general.

"Hang on", you may be thinking. "That misses the point. The point is that for any pair of behaviourally indistinguishable but deep-functionally transposed individuals *a* and *b*, such that *a* sees the world in way A and *b* sees it in way B, there is nothing to prevent A and B *themselves* from having been transposed, so that the deep-functional structure which in *a* supposedly gives rise to way A might, instead, have given rise to *a*'s seeing the world in way B, and vice versa. How could there be a *necessary* connection between a particular combination of qualia and a particular deep-functional structure?"

At first sight that may look like a serious renewal of the transposed qualia challenge to all forms of functionalism. Further reflection reveals it is based on a misconception. The deep variety of functionalism in question is certainly committed to there being two different ways of seeing colours, A and B. But it is also committed to there being *no more involved* in seeing colours in one of these ways than there is in having a certain deep-functional structure (whatever structure that may be). It thus rules out the possibility assumed in the objection. You may think it is obviously mistaken to claim there is no more involved in seeing colours in way A than there is in having the deep-functional structure in question; it may seem obvious to you that you just can't *get* qualia out of functions (an objection to be considered below). But the objection depends on a presupposition to that effect: it therefore begs the question against the functionalist.

6.8 "Qualia are intrinsic, not relational"

Reflecting on what seems to be the nature of qualia on the one hand, and what is distinctive about functionalism on the other, some philosophers have argued that functionalism cannot possibly do what it sets out to do: you can't get qualia out of functions. They put the point in various ways; the following is typical.

Functionalist accounts of the nature of mental states are *relational*. According to functionalism, whether or not an individual is in a given mental state depends on causal or other relations between that mental state and inputs, outputs and other mental states. It is then urged that the characters of conscious mental states – "qualia" – are not relational but "intrinsic". Each quale has its own determinate character and doesn't depend on its relations with anything else (see for example Levine 2001).

To see how functionalists can meet this objection we need first to recall that there is no need for them to find functional equivalents for descriptions of qualia. That project seems doomed in any case; but for reasons noted at §§4.2 and 6.5, neither physicalists in general nor functionalists in particular have to undertake it. Certainly they are required to explain how it is that there are such things as conscious experiences with their own special characters; but that does not force them to provide functional equivalents to descriptions of such experiences.

Associated with that is the Nagelian point that the *concepts* in terms of which we describe the character of our experiences are special, in that in order to have those concepts (which I am calling "viewpoint-relative"), it seems necessary for their users to have had, or at least to be capable of imaginatively constructing, the right kinds of experiences.

Now, functionalists maintain there is some functional explanation of *what it is* for something to be a subject of conscious experiences. Just what the details of this explanation might be is something still to be considered: some of the main proposals will be discussed in Chapter 8. But the explanation will certainly be relational in the sense that it will set out what relations between the components of a system must hold in order for it to be such a subject. It will have something like the following form:

> Being a subject of conscious experiences is a matter of being a system with such-and-such functional relationships, and for the system actually to have a conscious experience with whatever character it may be is for processes to occur in it which have so-and-so relations with the system's inputs, outputs and other states.

Since this is supposed to serve just as a schema or general pattern, it is almost totally uninformative! However, once the relevant relational conditions have been set out – once the "so-and-so"s and "such-and-such"s have been filled in – functionalists can maintain that *they provide scope for the use of viewpoint-relative concepts*. For if the functionalist account is sound, those conditions explain how it is that there *are* such things as conscious experiences.

Given a subject of conscious experiences, then, viewpoint-relative concepts can be applied to that subject's experiences. If subjects are cognitively sophisticated enough, they can apply the concepts themselves. But that is not necessary: others can apply them on their behalf. Now, nothing forces functionalists to concede that whoever applies those concepts must *know* which causal or other relations are involved in the functionalist account of the experiences. Functionalists say: "There can *be* no conscious experiences, no qualia, without the right functional relations." But nothing prevents them from adding: "*Descriptions* of experiences are not relational (or not manifestly so)." The special viewpoint-relative concepts are apt for describing and thinking about the character of experiences from the subject's point of view, so there is no reason why they should wear their causal or other functional underpinnings on their sleeves. That there should be such concepts seems unremarkable, given the differences between an observer's treating something (which happens to be a subject) as a thing to be observed and reported on, and the subject's own treatment of how the world strikes them. Acquiring those concepts does not require a knowledge of the functional basis for the existence of the experiences to which they nevertheless apply. And, of course, merely to have a particular sort of experience is enough to justify saying one has it.

Reflecting on those considerations, we can see how easy it is to assume that the *nature* of conscious experiences is not relational, hence how easy it is to assume, via ideas of zombies, transposed qualia and the like, that a functionalist account of their nature is not available even in principle. But if the above considerations are sound, the fact that experiences *seem* to be non-relational is no objection.

Those points also throw some light on the relations between physical and psychological descriptions and explanations. The fact that the latter have a place for the subject's own point of view helps to explain why they have features absent from the former.

6.9 Conclusion

Although some varieties of functionalism seem vulnerable to some of the objections discussed, others are resistant to them. On the other hand, we have not seen overwhelming reasons to accept a functionalist account of the mental. And we have hardly considered how functionalism can account for intentionality. That will be part of the task of Chapter 7.

Main points in Chapter 6
1. Functionalism originally appeared to be just a way of meeting objections to the psycho-physical identity thesis. Then it was suggested that functional relationships actually *constituted* the nature of mental states (§§6.1, 6.2).
2. Functionalism has no problems over multiple realizability: "We could be made of Swiss cheese and it wouldn't matter" (§§6.2, 6.3).
3. Lewis's proposal to use "Ramsey sentences" to define mental predicates is an interesting approach to dealing with, among other things, the problem of specifying inputs and outputs (§6.4).
4. Functionalists do not have to provide logical equivalents or definitions of statements about individual mental states (§6.5).
5. Two standard objections to functionalism appeal to "transposed qualia" and "absent qualia". Functionalists have the resources to reply to both (§§6.6, 6.7).
6. The objection that qualia are "intrinsic" and not relational overlooks the fact that what is fundamentally relational may strike the subject as intrinsic.

Further reading
For further introductory material on functional accounts of the mind see Block (ed.) (1980: "Introduction"), Dennett (1978a: xi–xxi), Smith & Jones (1986: 152–89) and Wilkes (1978: 54–66). For more advanced material see Armstrong (1968), Dennett (1978c), Fodor (1968, 1974), Lewis (1972, 1983), Putnam (1975c, 1975d) and Smart (1959).

Some varieties of functionalism are not covered here. For "machine functionalism" see Putnam (1960, 1967) and for "teleological (or evolutionary) functionalism" see Millikan (1986).

For a range of objections to functionalism see Block (1978), Chalmers (1996), Levine (2001) and McDowell (1985).

The possibility of transposed qualia is defended in Chalmers (1996) and (provided there are physical differences too) in Kirk (1994) and Shoemaker (1975, 1981b). It is attacked in Kirk (1981) and Dennett (1991).

The possibility of absent qualia is defended in Block (1980) and attacked in Dennett (1991), Kirk (1994, 1999) and Shoemaker (1981a).

7 More about thinking

Romeo loves Juliet. He tells her so. He spends as much time with her as he can, and when he can't be with her he sends her roses and emails. Naturally he spends a lot of time thinking about her. At the moment he is wondering whether to buy her a ring, although he has no particular ring in mind.

We have no trouble understanding how Romeo's roses and emails reach Juliet. But how can his *thoughts* get to her? How is it possible for a purely physical organism to have thoughts which reach out into the world, and may even be about things that don't exist? You don't have to feel drawn to dualism to find intentionality mysterious. We have already glanced at some of the main approaches to these questions; in this chapter we will go deeper. To start with we will look at two strongly opposed ways of explaining what it is for Romeo to think about Juliet.

7.1 Two opposed explanations of intentionality

If you had asked Plato, Aristotle, Locke, Hume or Kant, or for that matter the Wittgenstein of the *Tractatus*, they would have replied that to think about something involves having an "idea", "impression", or "representation" of that thing in your mind. To think about Juliet, Romeo must have an internal representation (idea, impression) of her. This "representation" is "mental", "internal", and of course *real*. On those assumptions, the intentionality of thoughts generally, and also of beliefs, desires, hopes, fears and other so-called "propositional attitudes", is a matter of being in some special relation to a "mental representation".

Ryle and the later Wittgenstein, in their different ways, reacted sharply against that approach, emphasizing the role of behaviour and behavioural dispositions. Their idea – revolutionary half a century ago – was that for Romeo to think about Juliet was for him to behave or be disposed to behave in certain ways in connection with Juliet – in fact, it was for him to be disposed to do just the sorts of things I mentioned at the start: to spend time with her, to whisper sweet nothings, to send her emails. They didn't deny there were things going on inside Romeo's head which were causally responsible for his behaviour and dispositions. But their view was that, whatever those internal processes might be, what really mattered was his behaviour and dispositions. As to the idea of internal "mental representations", that was just a sort of primitive superstition.

But there has been a counter-revolution. Today it is common to assume that thinking does after all require a "mental representation" of what is being thought about. On this account Romeo must indeed have a mental representation of Juliet, or an internal "symbol" which stands for her. The strongest version of this type of explanation is Jerry Fodor's hypothesis of the "Language of Thought" (LOT).

7.2 The LOT hypothesis

Plato suggested that thinking is "the inward dialogue carried on by the mind with itself". This idea involves only ordinary "natural" languages such as Greek or English, which we pick up by exposure to people speaking them, and whose utterances we can hear or see. One problematic implication is that non-human animals and human infants don't think. Fodor's idea of the Language of Thought avoids that difficulty. It is sharply distinct from the idea that thinking is just the use of an ordinary language.

Fodor's overall aim is to explain intentionality in a way consistent with both physicalism and a strongly realistic conception of beliefs, desires and other "propositional attitudes". According to this realistic conception beliefs, desires and the rest really exist and really have the properties normally ascribed to them. Notably they can be evaluated as true or false, and they play causal roles in the production of behaviour. In addition such intentional states are, on Fodor's account, not just part of folk psychology: they are to be covered by the laws of scientific psychology.

His core idea is this. Psychological descriptions and explanations apply to an organism on account of the workings within it of an "internal code" analogous to a computer's machine code (see §1.7). Suppose it occurs to the organism that foxes are dangerous. In order to have that belief it must have the concepts *fox* and *dangerous*. According to the LOT hypothesis this requires its internal code to possess predicates equivalent to the English words "fox" and "dangerous". For every belief which the organism is capable of entertaining there is a corresponding formula in its internal code. (It is a formula-*type*: analogous to a word capable of being used on many occasions.) And for each actual *episode* of believing there is a token of a LOT formula in an appropriate place in its brain. (This token is analogous to the actual utterance of an expression.) In Fodor's words: "For each episode of believing that P, there is a corresponding episode of having, 'in one's belief box', a mental representation which means that P" (1998: 8). Belief is just one of the relations in which a token of the internal code may stand to the organism. Another is desire; another is intention; another is hope . . . Just what sorts of relations these are is problematic; but for our purposes it will be enough to think of there being a "belief box", a "desire box", and so on, all appropriately connected to the rest of the organism. If an instance of the LOT formula meaning that *I have a cup of coffee* is in my belief box, it may, together with other attitudes, result in my taking a sip. If on the other hand a token of the same formula is in my desire box, it may cause me to go into a coffee bar.

Just as the sentences of a natural language are constructed from words and other constituents that can occur in indefinitely many other sentences, so the mental formulas of the internal code have their own "compositional structure". In Fodor's words:

> we could say that the LOT story amounts to the claims that (1) (some) mental formulas have mental formulas as parts; and (2) the parts are 'transportable': the same parts can appear in *lots* of mental formulas.   (1987: 137)

And the way in which complex formulas are built up from simpler ones ensures that, again as in a natural language, what a complex formula means is determined by what its simple constituents mean, and what a complex formula refers to (if to anything) is fixed by what its constituents refer to.

A key claim is that because each belief or desire is represented by a token formula of the LOT in the appropriate "box", the work of causing behaviour is done by the formula's purely *physical* properties – its shape would be a simple example (though probably wrong). Its *meaning* does no such causal work. The analogy with computers is close. What does the work in a computer is patterned electrical impulses acting on the circuits in the machine's arithmetic-logic unit. The fact that these electrical impulses are interpretable as instructions to add, subtract, multiply or compare numbers does not contribute to explaining their causal role. In Fodor's view, there is a comparable parallelism between the causal roles of the physical formulas of the LOT and the explanatory roles of the propositional attitudes that correspond to them. Suppose I believe that:

It will rain

and also that:

If it rains, then the match will be cancelled.

And suppose the result is that I end up believing that:

The match will be cancelled.

There is of course an explanation for my acquiring this last belief in terms of the *contents* or *meanings* of my beliefs. But according to Fodor this explanation works because those physical entities in the brain that are tokens of LOT formulas corresponding to *It will rain* and *If it rains, then the match will be cancelled* – formulas lodged in my "belief box" – actually *cause* a physical token of the formula which means that *the match will be cancelled* to be lodged in my belief box.

Fodor has always recognized that the LOT hypothesis strikes many philosophers as more or less absurd; but he has been impressed by a number of arguments. One is that when coming to a decision about a course of action, any organism whose behaviour is explicable in terms of beliefs and desires – any organism with a "psychology" – is able to consider a range of options. In order to do so, he holds, the organism must have a "representational system" capable of formulating each of a range of options. Such a system must, he thinks, have many of the features of a language. However, the internal code itself does not have to be *learnt*. According to Fodor it is either innate or develops without learning, like bones and teeth.

Fodor emphasizes arguments based on the supposed "productivity" and "systematicity" of intentional states. *Productivity* is the power to produce infinitely many, or at any rate indefinitely many, different items of a certain category. It seems that our thoughts have this sort of productivity. Each of us can entertain any of an indefinitely large number of thoughts. Consider, now, the productivity of a natural language: the fact that each speaker can produce indefinitely many acceptable sentences. We already have an explanation of this. Whole sentences are composed of "transportable" parts: words and other expressions that can figure in any number of different sentences. If we assume that beliefs, desires and other intentional states also have that sort of "combinatorial structure" – so that which belief it is, and its causal relations with other mental states, "depends on what elements it contains and how they are put together" (1987: 147) – then we have an *explanation* of the productivity of thought. This explanation amounts to the LOT hypothesis.

The *systematicity* of our ability to produce and understand sentences consists in the fact that if we can produce or understand one sentence with a certain structure, then we can also do so for indefinitely many different sentences with the same structure. If we can produce or understand "Romeo loves Juliet", for example, we can produce or understand many other sentences, including "Juliet loves Romeo", "Antonio loves Juliet" and so on. Fodor argues that the best explanation of this systematicity is, again, that intentional states themselves have a similar kind of "constituent structure". He summarizes:

> Linguistic capacities are systematic, and that's because sentences have constituent structure. But cognitive capacities

are systematic too, and that must be because *thoughts* have constituent structure. But if thoughts have constituent structure, the LOT is true.   (1987: 150f.)

7.3 Trouble for the LOT

We saw that a human infant's LOT is supposed to be not learnt, but "innate" in a broad sense that admits of time being taken for it to develop, as teeth and bones develop. The infant just "develops", without learning, a "representational system" that has the conceptual resources to translate *any* bit of humanly learnable language. Since possession of a "representational system" necessarily involves possession of the concepts in terms of which that system classifies things, Fodor acknowledges that this means that "the concept-learning task cannot coherently be interpreted as a task in which concepts are learned" (1975: 96). He recognizes that this is a highly problematic claim: many philosophers find it incredible.

It is widely accepted that for many concepts, if not all, grasping the concept requires grasping some theory. Suppose we concede for the sake of argument that there are "purely observational" concepts, such as, perhaps, *red*, *noisy*. Even so, many concepts applying to observable things are not purely observational. Such concepts make difficulties for the view that concepts are not learned: for "radical concept nativism", as Fodor calls it (1998). One source of examples is scientific theories. To have the concept *atom* seems impossible without knowing something about a theory explaining the nature of atoms and their theorized relations to other things. But this difficulty is not confined to highly theoretical concepts. Take the concept *doorknob*. Could anyone have that concept without knowing anything about doors, and knowing that they perform the function of covering entrances/exits in buildings and can be opened and shut? It is hard to see how.

It seems that supporters of the LOT hypothesis face a dilemma. Either they deny that grasping concepts requires grasping theories, contrary to what seems to be the case; or else they concede that possession of concepts requires knowledge of theories and give up the idea that concept-possession is innate or just a matter of tooth-like natural development.

Another difficulty arises in connection with Fodor's intention that the LOT hypothesis should provide a framework for a *scientific* psychology: one whose laws quantify over "*mental states that are specified under intentional description*; viz. among mental states that are picked out by reference to their contents", and are about causal relations among these states (1998: 7, original emphasis). The only methods we know of at present for discovering the contents of people's mental states are (a) observing their behaviour (including, sometimes, our own behaviour); or (b) whatever *non-*observational means enable a person to come to know their own mental states. Neither (a) nor (b) requires knowledge of, or access to, the hypothesized formulas of people's internal codes. (If it did, none of us would ever know anything about anyone's mental states, since no one has ever come across a formula of the LOT.) That makes it a puzzle how the contentfulness of internal code formulas could contribute to a scientific explanation of the contentfulness of mental states. If everything we know about the contentfulness of mental states comes from facts lying *outside* the hypothesized and so far undiscovered formulas, it is mysterious how the latter could come into the story at all.

That brings us to a further difficulty. The LOT hypothesis requires the internal code formulas themselves to be meaningful, to have contents; but exponents of the hypothesis do not agree on how they get their contents. (See the essays in Loewer & Rey 1991. Stephen Stich and others have concluded that there is no need to posit contents for the formulas: Stich 1983.)

7.4 "Symbolizing" representations

At this point we need to notice some distinctions, for the word "representation" is so flexible as to be ambiguous. *Non-mental* representation is pretty well unproblematic. Maps represent regions of the earth. Photographs represent people and scenes. Verbal descriptions represent anything you can describe. All these are typically concrete objects which convey information to us about this or that aspect of the world.

In those cases, the fact that a given concrete object represents something is not "intrinsic" to it. That is (to put a problematic idea as if it were unproblematic), it is not the nature of the concrete object *alone* that determines whether it represents anything, or what it represents. Suppose a child draws a wavy shape on a piece of paper, and it so happens that the outline matches that of Australia. Does that make the child's outline a map of Australia, even though the child knows nothing at all about Australia – doesn't even know about maps? Certainly the child's effort could be *used* as a map of Australia by someone who took the trouble to check that it was the right shape; but that surely doesn't make it a map of that continent. Similarly, an image on photographic film doesn't *represent* a particular person, or even a person at all, just because it could serve that purpose. It has to have been caused in the right way (recall §1.11, and see Putnam 1981: 1–5).

When it comes to *mental* representations things are not so straightforward. The expression seems to be used in more than one way, and the differences between these uses are not always noticed. Here are three relevant ways:

(i) *Everyday (or "folk") psychological representations.* Let's assume we reject eliminativism (see §3.9), behaviourism, and instrumentalism (§§5.6, 5.7), and that in some suitably broad and vague sense we really have beliefs, desires, intentions and other intentional states or "propositional attitudes". In other words, let's assume we are to that extent realists about intentional states. Since beliefs represent the world, just having beliefs can be described as "having mental representations". Similarly for desires, hopes, fears, since these also represent the world – not as it is, but as we desire, hope or fear it to be. That is a relatively unproblematic sense of "mental representation".

(ii) *Realizing representations.* Given the minimal intentional realism of (i), there must be *some* features of our internal states which provide for our having beliefs and the rest; and these internal features can (because they often are) themselves be described as representations. They are physical items that realize at least some aspects of our having beliefs, desires, or whatever it might be. That must *not* be taken to imply that these realizing representations resemble sentences, or that they are themselves meaningful or contentful. All it commits us to is that there are some sorts of physical structures that underlie the realities of our having beliefs and so on – with no commitments about the details of those structures.

(iii) *Symbolizing representations.* Consider the following piece of reasoning:

> To think (e.g.) that Marvin is melancholy is to represent Marvin in a certain way; viz. as being melancholy . . . But *surely we cannot represent Marvin as being melancholy except as we are in some or another relation to a representation of Marvin*; and . . . in particular, to a representation the content of which is *that* Marvin is melancholy.
>
> (Fodor 1981: 225, my italics)

This might perhaps have been construed as implying no more than is implied by our merely having beliefs, or at most no more than "realizing representations". But the context makes clear that Fodor is going crucially further. His claim is that these realizing representations *symbolize*, either by having meanings, like sentences in English or other "natural" languages, or by referring to things, as names and descriptions do. To be committed to the existence of such symbolizing representations is to adopt a basic tenet of what Fodor calls the Representational Theory of Mind. (The Representational Theory is entailed by the LOT hypothesis, but does not entail it.) He has expressed this tenet as follows:

(T) "Mental representations" are the primitive bearers of intentional content.   (1998: 7)

(T) implies that realizing representations (the underlying physical structures or processes) *are* symbolizing ones. Fodor takes it that these in-the-head items are contentful: they have meaning, and some of them refer to things.

The view encapsulated in (T) is often not clearly distinguished from commitment to minimal realism about intentional states (type (i)), and to the existence of realizing representations (type (ii)). Indeed, Fodor himself sometimes seems to assume that commitment to type (i) minimal intentional realism just *is* commitment to symbolizing representations. Yet it remains obscure why realizing representations should also be supposed to be symbolizing ones (see §§7.6–7.10).

7.5 Scepticism about compositional/constituent structure

The LOT doctrine can be seen as one kind of hypothesis about the nature of realizing representations: that they are also symbolizing. We have noted that the case for this view is not compelling. But there is scepticism about another crucial claim: that the formulas of the internal code have a "constituent structure" which mirrors the structure of the verbal expressions of beliefs, desires and so on. It strikes many philosophers as implausible that the relation between beliefs and realizing representations should be as straightforward as the LOT hypothesis has it.

Consider a favourite example of Dennett's: chess-playing computers. Their programs enable them to play well; and it is helpful to take up the "intentional stance" to them. When we do so, we are able to predict and explain their behaviour in such terms as that "It has a policy of getting its Queen out early". Such ascriptions of belief are in many ways similar to those we apply to other people. Yet although it is useful to make such ascriptions to chess-playing machines, the machine's program need not include any explicit internal sentence-like "representations" of the beliefs ascribed. Certainly there must be *something* about the machine's internal physical structure which warrants the ascription to it of that "attitude": there must be some sort of "realizing representation". But we don't seem justified in assuming that this realizing representation itself has a constituent structure mirroring its verbal expression. If we are not justified in making that assumption for chess-playing machines, how can we be justified in making it for people? Relations between the beliefs we ascribe on the one hand, and their realizing representations on the other, may be nothing like so direct as the LOT hypothesis requires, and as a number of philosophers who reject that hypothesis also assume.

In Chapter 5 we noticed reasons for giving up behaviourism and accepting that the nature of the internal processing matters. But we found no clear indications of just what sorts of internal processing are the right sorts. The LOT hypothesis purports to fill that gap – but in a way that critics regard as suspiciously neat. The original problem was to explain the fact that we have intentional states – beliefs, desires, intentions and so on – which (a) have content, in the sense that they are *about* things in the world; (b) are capable of being true or false (at least in the case of beliefs); and (c) contribute to causing behaviour. The "explanation" offered is that to each such intentional state of an individual there corresponds a token formula in that individual's LOT, which (a) has content; (b) is capable of being true or false; and (c) contributes to causing behaviour. Is that really an explanation or just a relocation of the original problem? It reminds one of the ancient explanation of human reproduction, according to which sperms were like tiny people.

Until a couple of decades ago (Fodor's *The Language of Thought* was first published in 1975) it was easy to assume that an explanation on those lines was the only kind possible. The only serious contender for a scientific approach to understanding the nature of cognition was based on the use of computers, and on the fact that information is often stored in forms with constituent structures. At that time it was reasonable to call the LOT hypothesis "the only game in town". But now the situation is different. *Connectionism* (including "parallel distributed processing" and "neural network modelling") is a radically different approach to the modelling of cognitive processes. It offers serious alternatives to the assumptions underlying the LOT hypothesis.

7.6 Connectionism

A range of significantly different approaches goes under the name "connectionism"; what's true for one isn't necessarily true for all. Here I will merely outline a sort of "minimal" connectionism. An important influence on these approaches is the knowledge that the brain consists of a vast number of interconnected cells, each capable of "firing" and thereby transmitting electrochemical impulses along outgoing fibres (axons) to other cells, which, when certain conditions are satisfied are caused to fire in their turn. Long-term memory storage depends on tiny modifications to these cells at the points where they are close to the filaments coming from other cells. Typically, the more signals a given neural pathway carries, the easier it becomes for signals to pass along it; and the less it is used, the harder it is for signals to pass.

However, connectionism is not primarily aimed at modelling the actual workings of the brain, even though its methods naturally lend themselves to modelling vital aspects of brain function. In general it aims at providing rather more generalized models of cognitive processing.

The basic conception, then, is of a large number of relatively simple units, all connected to one another and sending signals along one-way channels. At any given time each unit has a certain "activation value", determined by its inputs and its value prior to that time. Typically, like a neurone, it will transmit signals only when its activation value crosses a certain threshold. Some of the units receive inputs from outside the system; others transmit outputs to external items of one sort or another. If the system is simply being modelled on a computer, the outputs will appear on a screen. If it is controlling a robot, the outputs will cause the robot to move. Between the input units and the output units there are a number of layers of "hidden units". Depending on the nature of the connections, a signal's arrival at a given unit may tend to cause that unit to be activated, or alternatively to be deactivated.

So at any moment there is a certain total pattern of activation values among the individual units of the network. This overall pattern is constantly changing over time, as quantities of signals are transmitted across the network. Just how it changes depends on the following main factors: the original pattern of activation values; the successive patterns of inputs received by the system from its environment; the strengths of the connections among the units; the rules (determined by the experimenter) according to which the activation value of each unit is modified by its inputs and in turn affects its outputs; and the rules according to which connection strengths (or "weights") are modified.

This last feature of the system ensures that in the course of time the strengths of the connections from unit to unit will change. Typically, as with neurones in the brain, the greater the activity along a given pathway, the easier it gets for signals to pass along it, and the less the activity, the harder it gets. But at any given time it is the total pattern of connection strengths (the system's "connectivity") which ensures that a particular pattern of input brings about a particular modification to the pattern of activation of units throughout the system. The result is that *the current pattern of connection strengths determines how the system will behave on receipt of a given pattern of inputs*. We can therefore say that in a connectionist system, *information* is represented not by sentences but by the total distribution of connection strengths.

In a connectionist system appropriately hooked up to "sense receptors", the way the pattern of connectivity evolves through time as a result of successive input patterns can be thought of as the system's *acquiring* information about its environment. Note that each unit's behaviour is determined entirely by the inputs it receives from whichever other units are directly connected to it. There is no central control monitoring the state of each unit.

Such models promise to explain many psychological phenomena, including pattern-recognition, "association of ideas", all aspects of learning, concept-possession and attention.

7.7 Connectionism, the LOT and psychology

If the acquisition, storage and processing of information can be usefully modelled by connectionist systems, is there any reason to continue taking the LOT idea seriously? Clearly connectionist modelling presents a serious challenge to the LOT hypothesis. Not only is it a fruitful alternative way of thinking about information reception, storage and processing. It seems to avoid two big problems for sentence-based or "classical" approaches, problems I have not yet mentioned.

One is that of "belief fixation": explaining how it is that, as an organism interacts with its environment, it is constantly acquiring new beliefs and losing old ones. The information coming in from an organism's sense organs is not in anything like sentence form; it does not seem to have constituent structure. Yet according to the LOT hypothesis the alleged mental representations do have that structure. Somehow or other, then, sensory inputs have to be transduced into LOT formulas; and the hypothesis is silent on how that can be done. Nor has classical AI come up with any convincing suggestions. Connectionism, in contrast, offers plausible schemes for getting from sensory inputs to stored information. No transduction into compositionally structured representations is involved.

The other problem is really a cluster of more or less closely related difficulties. They arise in connection with the modelling of situations in which people are able very swiftly both to retrieve relevant information and to ignore irrelevant information. If I have mislaid my notebook I try to think where I have been since I last used it. I don't waste time thinking about where I originally acquired it or how much it cost. It is difficult to devise programs for solving such problems if the information is stored in any of the ways envisaged in classical AI: attempted solutions run into problems of "combinatorial explosion". Connectionist models, in contrast, provide for quick solutions. (This cluster of problems has come to be called the "frame problem", although that name strictly applies only within a narrow area. See for example Dennett 1978c.)

Defenders of the LOT hypothesis are willing to concede that connectionism may explain the "neural (or 'abstract neurological') structures in which Classical cognitive architecture is implemented" (Fodor & Pylyshyn 1988: 3). But they insist that connectionists need "to show that the processes which operate on *the representational states* of an organism are those which are specified by a Connectionist architecture", and that it is "no use at all" just showing that "nonrepresentational" states constitute a connectionist network. That would "*leave open* the question whether the mind is such a network *at the psychological level*" (1988: 10. See also Stich 1983: 210). In support of their "classical" approach, according to which "the kind of computing that is relevant to cognition involves operations on . . . structured symbolic expressions" (Fodor & Pylyshyn 1988: 4f.), they appeal to the reasoning based on the "systematicity of thought" that we considered earlier (§7.2).

It is open to connectionists to reply that there doesn't have to be a "psychological level" of the kind Fodor and Pylyshyn suppose: a level of description and explanation inhabited by *symbolizing* representational states rather than just by *realizing* ones. The debate continues.

7.8 Intentionality in other animals

Considering other animals than ourselves may help us to get a fresh view of our problems. I will start with something very humble, the tick (an example I have used elsewhere):

After mating, the female climbs to the tip of a twig on some bush. There she clings at such a height that she can drop upon small mammals that may run under her, or be brushed off by larger animals. The eyeless tick is directed to this watchtower by a general photosensitivity of her skin. The approaching prey is revealed to the blind and deaf highwaywoman by her sense of smell. The odour of butyric acid, that emanates from the skin glands of all mammals, acts on the tick as a signal to leave her watchtower and hurl herself downwards. If, in doing so, she lands on something warm – a fine sense of temperature betrays this to her – she has reached her prey, the warm-blooded creature. It only remains for her to find a hairless spot. There she burrows deep into the skin of her prey and slowly pumps herself full of warm blood. Experiments with artificial membranes and fluids other than blood have proved that the tick lacks all sense of taste. Once the membrane is perforated, she will drink any fluid of the right temperature.

(Jakob von Uexkull, *Umwelt und Innenwelt der Tiere* (1909), quoted in McFarland (ed.) 1987: 449f.)

It would be easy to ascribe beliefs, desires and intentions to this creature. Why did she climb the twig? To get to a suitable observation post. Why did she wait there? Because she wanted to find a suitable source of food. Why did she "hurl herself downward"? Because she believed a suitable warm-blooded creature was below. Why did she burrow into its skin? Because she intended to suck its blood. However, her behaviour was actually just the activation of a sequence of reflexes. The need for nourishment triggered twig-climbing, which in turn was directed by a simple phototropic reflex. Butyric acid vapour was the next stimulus, and caused her to release her grip on the twig. Warmth triggered burrowing, and the proximity of her target's skin triggered her blood-sucking reflex. Once we know her behaviour was caused in that way, we abandon the project of explaining it in terms of beliefs and desires. We *could* perhaps construct a belief–desire explanation of even a piano's behaviour; but since we know how it works, that project would be pointless. If behaviour is explicable in terms of such reflexes, then it is not the result of beliefs, desires, or other intentional states.

How much more complicated does a system have to be to qualify as a genuine subject of beliefs and desires? You might suggest that it qualifies if it can learn. A piano cannot learn; while even fruit-flies learn to find their way to familiar spots. But one kind of learning is just the acquisition of new reflexes; and surely behaviour that is wholly explicable in terms of reflexes, whether permanent or acquired, is not the result of beliefs or desires. Nor do we automatically get learning if the links from stimulus to response are somehow loosened, so that it becomes only probable, not certain, that a given stimulus is followed by a given response. Genuine believing and desiring are just not a matter of simple stimulus–response arrangements.

A key consideration is that believing is at least in part a matter of acquiring *information* – and this must be information that the organism itself can *use*: information that is "for it", in a useful phrase of Dennett's (1969: 46f.). Cameras and video recorders are devices that *we* use to acquire and store information. But the information on their films and tapes is not something *they* can use. It is information for us, not for them. In order for information to be *for* the organism, or more generally for the system, the system itself must be able to use it. When we reflect on the implications of those points, they suggest the following ideas.

In order for a system to be able to use information it must be able to retain it: it must have some sort of memory. (Contrast a system working wholly by reflexes: there is no provision for it to store information. The piano remembers nothing.) To be able to use information it must have goals or objectives of some kind, even if it cannot describe those goals. A cat chasing a mouse doesn't have to say anything to itself – it doesn't say, "Ha! A mouse: must chase it". But it does have goals or objectives that cannot be assimilated to mere needs or drives. Even ticks have needs and drives: they need warm blood; lack of nourishment drives them up twigs. The cat's needs and drives cause it to have more immediate goals, such as catching the mouse (as we, but not the cat, would put it). If a system altogether lacks goals or objectives, then nothing could explain its doing one thing rather than another; which is a way of saying that it doesn't act on the basis of information. Any information there may be inside it is not, after all, information *for it*. If on the other hand the system does use information in that way, as a basis for guiding its behaviour, then it must be able to tell how things are going: for example it must be able to tell whether or not it is getting closer to, or further away from, its current objective. That in turn implies that it must be able to *interpret* incoming information. (The cat hears a squeak and interprets it as mouse-caused rather than, say, child-caused.) And now we come to a crucial further point. If the system is able to tell what's going on with a view to guiding its behaviour, it must also be capable of *deciding* what to do next – even if this is only a minimal or rudimentary kind of deciding. This implies that it can, however minimally, *assess* its situation.

In this way the idea of a system capable of acquiring and retaining information which it can use to guide its behaviour – a system which *perceives* some of the things around it – brings together and integrates a whole complex of capacities, notably the following:

(i) to acquire and store information which it can use;
(ii) to use stored information as a basis for controlling its behaviour;
(iii) to have goals or objectives;
(iv) to interpret information;
(v) to assess its situation;
(vi) to choose between alternative courses of action on the basis of stored information.

"Information" in this context must be understood in a very general sense. Obviously it doesn't have to be in verbal form; but it needn't be in pictorial form either: our consideration of connectionism has shown that information *can* be acquired and processed, and be a causal factor in the production of behaviour, if it is something as abstract as the acquisition of a certain pattern of connection strengths.

It is vital that the capacities listed be *integrated*, so that the events which constitute the system's acquiring information about its environment have appropriate effects on its processes of interpretation, assessment and decision-making. Contrast the pantomime horse discussed in Chapter 5. What passes for "its" acquisition of information is nothing but the acquisition of information by Front Legs and Back Legs. Information gets inside the pantomime horse all right; but it is not information for it, just for its two operators. Nor are there any processes that could be counted as its own assessment or decision-making: there is only the operators' assessment and decision-making.

I will call any system which has this complex of capacities a *deciding system*, or alternatively a system with the *basic package* of capacities. I would argue that this package forms a unity, in that a system cannot have any one of them without having the rest; but I will not pursue that claim here.

One reason for sketching this idea of a deciding system is that I think it is a useful approach to answering an important question raised in Chapter 5: what conditions have to be satisfied if an organism is to be counted as capable of *aboutness*? It is also a useful approach to answering a more general question: what can we say about the nature of the internal processing, given that it matters? But an objection might have occurred to you. The capacities in the basic package are themselves described in intentional terms. If I then attempt to explain what aboutness or intentionality is on the basis that the basic package is either necessary or sufficient for intentionality, isn't that blatantly question-begging? It would certainly have been question-begging if I had been aiming to *define* intentionality in terms of the basic package. But that is not my aim. Instead, I think the idea of the basic package helps to illuminate the nature and structure of systems whose behaviour can reasonably be said to be "about" things. For that purpose it is not necessary for the basic package to be explained without using intentional notions. There is a further point: the notions used in explaining the capacities involved in the basic package seem less problematic than the central intentional notions of believing, desiring and intending.

The blackbird's behaviour as it searched for, found and chopped up a worm for eating could reasonably be said to be "about" the worm. I think any deciding system's behaviour can properly be described as being about at least some of the things it deals with; and further that it is *only* deciding systems which can properly be so described; but it would be out of place to defend those claims here. Notice that, thanks to the moderate realism of everyday psychology, the notion of a deciding system provides a useful framework for filling the gap left by behaviourism. Behaviourism fails to acknowledge the need for a system to have the "right kinds of internal processing". Whatever the details may be, the right kinds of internal processing will be those that ensure the system is genuinely a deciding system rather than a mere imitation such as the panto-mime horse or Block's machines.

However, what mainly concerns us in this chapter is not the aboutness of behaviour in general; it is the aboutness of thoughts – of believing, wanting, intending and the rest. One route to this is the aboutness of uses of language.

7.9 The intentionality of language

We noticed in Chapter 5 that behaviourists regard the use of language as just a special kind of behaviour. Behaviourism's defects make it easy to be distracted from the importance of this thought. True, the right sorts of behaviour and dispositions alone are not enough; the internal processing must be of the right sort. But it remains a fact that the use of language *is* just one kind of behaviour, even though it is so special and so hugely important in our lives.

Pretend for a moment that the basic package provides sufficient indication of what qualifies a system's non-linguistic behaviour as being about things in the world. On that basis it is hard to see why there should be a special problem over the aboutness of *linguistic* behaviour. In particular there is no pressure to make the aboutness of linguistic behaviour depend on the aboutness of internal "symbolizing" representations. This point may become clearer if we imagine some of our remote hominid ancestors.

Suppose a small community of these hominids gets to develop a variety of sign language. We know that sign languages have syntax and expressive power comparable to spoken languages; and sign language is a helpful way to illustrate my points because producing gestures is easier to see as "just another kind of behaviour" than speaking is. Suppose, then, that the following conventions hold in the sign language of this particular little community:

(i)   raising one's forefinger is a way of referring to Anno, an individual;

(ii) raising one's second finger refers to Banno;

(iii) raising the third finger refers to Canno;

(iv) straightening one's arm at the elbow means that whoever is being referred to is away;

(v) bending one's arm at the elbow says that whoever is referred to
     is in the cave.

Bending an arm with the second finger raised, then, means that
Canno is in the cave. So when Banno makes that gesture in Anno's
presence, Anno is thereby caused to acquire the belief that Canno is
in the cave. However, as it happens, *Banno himself doesn't yet
know what his gesture means*: it's just a piece of behaviour he has
recently copied from Danno. That being so, there can be no
question of Banno's production of that gesture having had anything
to do with any internal symbolizing representation which somehow
mirrors its structure: for him, bending your arm with the second
finger raised is *just* a striking bit of behaviour.

Eventually Banno picks up the little community's language.
Now, according to the LOT hypothesis, Banno's LOT works in
tandem with his use of this sign language. In particular, his ability to
use a raised little finger to refer to Canno is claimed to *depend* on
his having a special internal item that also refers to Canno; and his
ability to convey the message that whoever it may be is in the cave
is supposed to *depend* on his having a special internal symbol, or
predicate of the LOT, which means that so-and-so is in the cave. But
when we reflect on how Banno actually picks up this community's
language, those ideas seem not just to involve pointless duplication:
they seem at best to get things the wrong way round. Banno
obviously doesn't need a symbolizing representation in order to be
able to extend his arm or raise a finger. He does that *before* he
knows what the gesture means.

And he can pick up the language bit by bit. For example he can
imitate the others in his family, and gradually get the hang of using
these gestures to do these jobs. There is a time when he has no idea
that the gestures perform the functions they do; there is a later time
when he knows very well what they do; there is also an intermediate period when he knows *something* about what *some* of them do.
But picking up the functions of these gestures, and how the different components of the signs can be combined, seems to be a similar
sort of process to that by which he imitates others' fish-catching or
bees'-nest-opening behaviour, and gets the hang of how to spear
fish or extract honey. He seems to get the point of spearing fish and
extracting honey without benefit of an internal symbol. Why, then,

can't he get the point of making the motions required for his community's sign language without benefit of such symbols? This seems to be a hard question for exponents of the LOT hypothesis – especially now that connectionism offers an alternative type of explanation of cognitive processes.

In general, the above considerations suggest (no more: we cannot pursue all the likely objections and qualifications) that the aboutness of language is just a special case of the aboutness of non-linguistic behaviour, and – crucially – does not depend on the presence of internal symbolizing representations.

Notice too that the sign-language example seems to block the LOT friends' appeal to the *systematicity* of our production and understanding of sentences. Our signers' outward behaviour is certainly systematic: being able to produce and understand the gesture which means that *Anno is in the cave* involves also being able to produce and understand the gesture which means *Canno is in the cave*, as well as the one which means that *Anno is away*. But if, as suggested by the considerations we noticed, such abilities do not depend on the workings of internal symbolizing representations whose structure and meanings correspond to the outward gestures, then the argument from systematicity is extremely weak. And if you suspect that our little community's language is too limited to serve the purpose, reflect that it can be extended in various ways, for example by introducing gestures for negation and conjunction – which immediately provides for indefinitely many well-formed sentences. Why should the ability to produce and use those sentences require corresponding internal processes – any more than, say, the ability to build indefinitely many different sorts of houses from bricks and other components requires builders to have "little houses in their heads": corresponding internal processes with similar structures?

7.10 Conclusion

The philosophical problems of intentionality are a tangled jungle, haunted by strange beasts. Plenty of promising ideas, but not much agreement on which, if any, is the best approach. To end this chapter, and hoping it may help you find your bearings in the jungle, I will emphasize four points.

First, there continues to be fundamental disagreement over how to answer this question: is intentionality mainly a matter of *behavioural* relations with the rest of the world, or is it mainly a matter of the nature of the *internal* states of the subject? This disagreement is at its most dramatic in the contrast between behaviourism and the LOT hypothesis. We have seen reasons to modify behaviourism to take account of the nature of the internal processing; but the modified view still puts most weight on external relations (§7.8–7.9). We have also seen reasons for scepticism over the LOT hypothesis (§§7.4–7.7).

Secondly, various forms of *functionalism* continue to be influential. The idea that what distinguishes mental states is their "functional" relations with sensory inputs, behavioural outputs and other inner states has much appeal, even though it may not work in exactly the form I have just stated it. Much of the complexity of the intentionality jungle arises from the multiplicity of attempts to refine that original idea.

Thirdly, keep in mind that the central notions of *representation*, *content* and *concept* are either very loose ones based in everyday psychology, or to some extent technical terms in philosophy and psychology. It's not as if nature herself forced these concepts on us, as perhaps she forces on us concepts like *gold* or *hydrogen*. Questions like "What is it for a mental state to have content?" or "Do animals have concepts?" seem more like questions about the best conventions for using those words than questions of fact.

Finally, in spite of disagreements and uncertainties, the main accounts of intentionality are such that there seems no serious reason to suppose it cannot be accommodated by physicalism. Certainly there are reasons for thinking that intentional notions cannot be *defined* in purely physical terms. Nor do many accounts easily provide for scientific *laws* governing intentional states. Still, all the accounts we have seen would be adequate to explain how the mental logically *supervenes* on the physical; and that is all that is necessary for physicalism (see §§3.10–3.12). In this respect the case of intentionality contrasts with the case of consciousness, as we shall see.

Main points in Chapter 7

1. We focused on two opposed conceptions of intentionality: one behaviour-based, one invoking mental representations in a special "symbolizing" sense (§§7.1, 7.2, 7.4, 7.8–7.9).

2. If Fodor's LOT hypothesis is sound, it solves the main problems of intentionality. But it is open to serious objections (§§7.2, 7.3).

3. There are reasons to be sceptical about both the "symbolizing" conception of mental representation and the idea that the compositional/constituent structure of *expressions* of thought is mirrored by underlying physical events (§§7.4, 7.5).

4. The LOT hypothesis is no longer "the only game in town". Connectionist models of mental functioning offer a promising radical alternative (§§7.6, 7.7).

5. The idea of a "deciding system" provides a basis for answering questions about "aboutness", and about what kinds of internal processing are necessary for genuine thinking and feeling (§7.8).

6. The intentionality of language can be explained without appealing to "symbolizing" representations (§7.9).

Further reading

Behaviour-based approaches to explaining intentionality were examined in Chapter 5: see the suggestions for further reading at the end of that chapter.

Approaches to explaining intentionality via mental representations in the "symbolizing" sense are ancient. (Dennett says "Descartes doubted almost everything *but* this": 1978c: 121f.) Recent works that presuppose the symbolizing sense (not clearly distinguished from the other senses) include Fodor (1998) and Horgan & Tienson (1996).

On the LOT see Fodor (1975, 1987: esp. "Postscript", reprinted in Lycan (ed.) 1990: 282–99). See also Churchland & Churchland (1983), Dennett (1978b), Loewer & Rey (eds) (1991) and Stich (1983: esp. ch. 3).

On connectionism see Bechtel and Abrahamsen (1991), Clark (1989), Copeland (1993: 207–47) and Ramsey *et al.* (eds) (1991). For the argument that connectionism can at most implement psychology see Fodor & Pylyshyn (1988). For the claim that connectionism is inconsistent with folk psychology see Ramsey *et al.* (1991) and other essays in Ramsey *et al.* (eds) (1991).

8 More about feeling

Romeo still loves Juliet. And although he thinks about her a lot, of course he also has feelings about her. That his feelings should be *about* her may by now be a little less puzzling. But what is it for him to have feelings? If intentionality remains a source of perplexity and controversy, so does consciousness.

Yet there is a significant difference between these components of the mind–body problem. In spite of disputes over which is the best approach to the naturalization of intentionality, it is widely agreed that the approaches examined in Chapter 7 help to demystify it. With consciousness the situation is different. The question of what it takes for there to be "something it is like" to have perceptual and other experiences still resists that sort of illumination. You may well be inclined to agree with Thomas Nagel's remark that with consciousness, the mind–body problem "seems hopeless". You might even be tempted by what is sometimes called "mysterianism": the view that the hard-wiring of human brains makes us forever incapable of understanding the solution to the mind–body problem (Colin McGinn 1991). A related but less pessimistic view is that the mind–body problem will not be solved until we have worked out a whole new science (Nagel 1998).

In this chapter we will look at the main accounts of consciousness current today. Some are varieties of functionalism or even behaviourism. To conclude the main body of the book I will sketch a fresh approach which I believe is promising. I don't think we should give up hope yet.

8.1 Kinds of consciousness

The kind of consciousness that chiefly raises problems beyond those posed by intentionality is *phenomenal* consciousness, which Nagel picks out with his example of the bat. Most of the accounts to be examined in this chapter aim to explain what phenomenal consciousness is.

Perceptual consciousness typically involves consciousness *of* something when it is perceived. As I walk down the street I am conscious of other people walking about, of the sound of cars and voices, of the smell of roasting coffee beans from an open door, and much else. Perceptual consciousness brings phenomenal consciousness with it: there is something it is like to see the people, smell the coffee roasting, and so on. However, not all phenomenal consciousness is also perceptual, as the case of dreaming illustrates.

Neither phenomenal consciousness nor perceptual consciousness *of* things seems to be the same as consciousness *that* . . . I am conscious/aware *that* I am typing blue letters on a white screen. I am also conscious *of* various other things, such as the slight hissing of my computer and the feel of the desk under my forearms. But I don't think I am also conscious *that* I am hearing the hiss or feeling the desk.

Finally there is consciousness as opposed to unconsciousness. In this sense we are conscious when awake and unconscious when asleep or knocked out – even if we are having phenomenally conscious experiences such as dreams. Being conscious in this sense is sometimes contrasted with "state"-consciousness. The idea is that it is one thing for the subject to be conscious, something else for the subject's *states* to be conscious. That distinction seems sound enough; but note that it is possible to approach the problem of so-called state-consciousness via an investigation into what it takes for the subject as a whole to be phenomenally or perceptually conscious (see §§8.8–8.11).

8.2 Sartre and Wittgenstein

Both Sartre and Wittgenstein wrote much about consciousness that is instructive and thought-provoking. Although their conceptions of philosophy differ in many ways, their approaches to consciousness are similar in an important respect. Both lay great emphasis on our *attitude* to beings like ourselves.

According to Sartre, when we are interacting with other people we normally *see them as conscious*. As he puts it, we see each person as a "for-itself" (*pour-soi*). However, we can also see other people as things, each as an "in-itself" (*en-soi*). Our attitude to another person is different from, and irreducible to, the attitude we have to an in-itself. But Sartre was no dualist. We have that attitude not because each person has a Cartesian mind, a special kind of "psychic object" linked up to the body. In his view there is nothing over and above the body, although it does have these two "aspects": as for-itself and as in-itself. He remarks that "there are no 'psychic phenomena' there to be united with the body. There is nothing *behind* the body. But the body is wholly 'psychic'" (1958: 305).

What concerns us here is not Sartre's general reflections on what it is like to be human, or what is characteristic of specifically human consciousness, interesting though those reflections are. What concerns us is anything he might have to contribute towards explaining *what it is* for there to be conscious systems in the first place. Unfortunately he is not focused on that question. He just takes for granted that there are these special entities, these "for-itself"s. Now, he rejects behaviourism, which would otherwise have provided some basis for his line. So perhaps he assumes either that there is no problem over what it takes for something to be a for-itself, or that he doesn't need to tackle the problem. There still is a problem, though, if we reject behaviourism and accept that the nature of the internal processing matters. Suppose we encountered a Block machine in conditions where its outward appearance, like its behaviour, resembled that of a normal human being. No doubt we would *see it as conscious*; but that wouldn't make it conscious. That we are accustomed to see others as conscious is a highly important fact; but it cannot be the whole story.

Wittgenstein remarked that:

> only of a living human being and what resembles (behaves like) a living human being can one say: it has sensations, it sees; is blind; hears; is deaf; is conscious or unconscious.
>
> (1953: sec. 281; see also secs 283, 360)

Presumably he isn't saying that behavioural resemblance is *sufficient*: he is no behaviourist. But he is saying it is in some way necessary. However, he doesn't insist on close behavioural resemblance. It makes no sense to say a stone is in pain, he says. "How could one so much as get the idea of ascribing a *sensation* to a *thing*? One might as well ascribe it to a number!" But "now look at a wriggling fly and at once these difficulties vanish and pain seems able to get a foothold here . . ." (sec. 284). When it comes to human beings the situation is reversed. It's not that we have difficulty understanding how they could be conscious. We can't make sense of the idea that they might *not* be conscious:

> But can't I imagine that the people around me are automata, lack consciousness, even though they behave in the same way as usual? . . . But just try to keep hold of this idea in the midst of your ordinary intercourse with others, in the street, say!
>
> (sec. 420)

If Wittgenstein's point is that human appearance and human behaviour are alone sufficient to guarantee the presence of consciousness, our examination of behaviourism has suggested reasons to the contrary (Ch. 5). If he is attacking the zombie idea – which he would certainly have rejected – and means that the difficulty of actually *treating* putative zombies as anything but normal conscious human beings settles the matter, it is not only the friends of zombies who will insist that that is not enough.

8.3 Dennett on "Multiple Drafts" and "Joycean machines"

With the aim of weakening the grip of the Cartesian Theatre model of the mind, Dennett introduces two new metaphors – of "Multiple Drafts" and "Joycean machines" – which he hopes better explain the nature of consciousness.

"Multiple Drafts"

It is widely accepted that mental activity involves a vast number of parallel processes. In perception, inputs from the senses are simultaneously elaborated, modified and interpreted by specialized subsystems, along parallel pathways distributed throughout the brain. There is no "headquarters" or "inner sanctum within the brain, arrival at which is the necessary or sufficient condition for conscious experience" (Dennett 1991: 106). Instead there are many "events of content-fixation"; and although these occur at precise times and places, their occurrence is not sufficient for consciousness. In fact:

> it is a confusion, . . . to ask [of one of them] *when it becomes conscious*. These distributed content-discriminations yield . . . something *rather like* a narrative stream or sequence . . . at any point there are multiple "drafts" of narrative fragments at various stages of editing in various places in the brain.
>
> (1991: 113, original emphasis)

What makes some of these "feature detections or discriminations", these "content-fixations", conscious? Dennett introduces a further metaphor, "probing": "Probing this stream [of Multiple Drafts] at different places and times produces different effects, produces different narratives from the subject" (1991: 113, cf. 135f.). What is probing? His examples suggest it is a sort of verbal self-questioning. You won't like that if you think consciousness doesn't require language. But if it isn't a linguistic act, what is it? Unfortunately Dennett's answer is not clear.

"Joycean machines"

The point of Dennett's second main metaphor emerges when we consider how evolution has equipped the brains of primates such as the great apes and ourselves. This sort of brain:

> consists of a conglomeration of specialist circuits designed to perform particular tasks in the economy of primate ancestors: looming-object detectors wired to ducking mechanisms, some-one-is-looking-at-me detectors wired to friend-or-foe-or-food discriminators wired to their appropriate further subroutines.
>
> (1991: 188)

How is the system as a whole controlled? Dennett notes that the scientific consensus favours models of the system's architecture whereby behaviour results from competition between specialized subsystems or "demons". However, such a system lacks the capacity to plan ahead. Human minds go beyond the basic primate kit; they can both reflect on what is currently happening and consider what might happen next. Dennett suggests this difference is not to be looked for in the neurological "hardware" we share with other primates. Instead it is a sort of "software" that we acquire via our culture. Human culture has evolved a complex system of "habits", crucially including those which constitute human language. Infants pick up this software – these habits – as they grow up. Among other things they learn to talk not only to others, but to themselves. Their spoken or unspoken monologues are like the flow of instructions and data through a standard computer ("Joycean" after James Joyce's *Ulysses*, dominated by the main character's unspoken monologues). So:

> I hereby declare that YES, my theory is a theory of conscious-ness. Anyone or anything that has such a virtual machine as its control system is conscious in the fullest sense, and is conscious *because* it has such a virtual machine.
>
> (1991: 281, original emphasis)

However, as we saw when considering his response to the zombie idea (§4.10), he rejects the thought that consciousness is "a special all-or-nothing property that sunders the universe into two vastly different categories" (1991: 447).

The idea that consciousness is provided for by the serial software of a "Joycean machine" implemented in hard-wired parallel archi-tecture is suggestive, but not trouble-free. For one thing, even if the hardware–software contrast helps to bring out the contrast between innate neural inheritance and culturally acquired "habits", it cannot be of fundamental theoretical importance since in principle any software-induced virtual machine could have been hard-wired. Nor does the parallel–serial contrast seem theoretically relevant, since anything a hard-wired parallel architecture can do can be done by a serial machine (as Dennett himself points out). When we keep in mind that possession of a Joycean machine is just a matter of a complex of "habits", Dennett's theory of conscious-ness threatens to boil down to the claim that a system is conscious just in case it is a language-user.

8.4 Pure representationalism

Many conscious experiences are representational. If I hear the sound of a car rushing past the house, that experience represents a car – even if there is no car there to be represented. If I dream I am flying, my dream experience represents me as flying. Now, we saw in Chapter 7 that in spite of disagreements over how to explain representation, the main rival accounts do at least remove the worry that it might be an ultimate mystery. So if we could explain the character of experiences – their phenomenality, the fact that there is something it is like to have them – in terms of their being representational, such an explanation would inherit the demystifying virtue of accounts of mental representation. What had appeared to be two distinct components of the mind–body problem – intentionality and consciousness – would have been reduced to one. That would be an enormous simplification.

Many philosophers today have adopted that view (including Dretske 1995, Tye 1995. See also McDowell 1985, 1994. Dennett has always favoured an approach on these lines: "First content, then consciousness": 1991: 457). Note particularly that these philosophers are not just saying that phenomenally conscious states *are* representational. What gives their position its interest is the claim that a state's being conscious or phenomenal involves no *more* than being representational. As Tye puts it, "phenomenal character can be *identified* with representational content of a certain sort" (1995: 15, my emphasis). I will call this position "pure representationalism".

The advantages of explaining consciousness in terms of representation are obvious, assuming we have a satisfactory approach to explaining representation. As we saw in Chapter 7, the most promising approaches to explaining representation do so on the basis that our mental states represent things on account of their causal relations to them. But there are difficulties.

An important difficulty is that experiences which are indistinguishable by the subject may be caused in significantly different ways. An experience subjectively like that of seeing a gold nugget may be caused by a piece of fool's gold; an experience like seeing a meteor may be caused by a neurosurgeon fiddling about with your visual cortex. Conceivably, then, *all* your experiences of a certain kind might be caused in a way that was non-standard relative to the

way it is typically caused with the rest us. Suppose there is a population which has typically encountered only fool's gold in situations
where we typically encounter real gold. Then pure representation-
alists face a dilemma. If they accept that representational content
depends on external causal relations, their view commits them to
maintaining that – since what is represented is different in the two
cases – the experience of seeing fool's gold *cannot* be phenomenally
just like that of seeing real gold, contrary to what we surely know.
The other alternative is to abandon the view that representational
content depends on external causal relations, in which case they
have to offer an alternative account of what it takes for a state to
represent something. (On "externalism" see §9.3.)

8.5 Higher-order perception

According to John Locke, "Consciousness is the perception of what
passes in a Man's own Mind" (*Essay* II.i.19). This is a tempting
idea, but it tends to force our thinking into the treacherous Cartesian Theatre model, where a little person inside the head witnesses
a parade of mental events. However, computer programs enable
machines to "scan" or "monitor" some of their own internal processes. Perhaps that is a better model for thinking about what Kant
called "inner sense". David Armstrong has suggested:

> If we make the materialist identification of mental states with
> material states of the brain, we can say that introspection is a
> self-scanning process in the brain. The scanning operation may
> itself be scanned, and so on . . .   (1968: 324)

He makes clear that the crucial point about this "scanning" is that it
is a matter of *getting information* about the system's own mental
states. Unfortunately we are able to get information unconsciously
as well as consciously, for example by "subliminal perception". So
this approach needs further development if it is to be persuasive.

8.6 Higher-order thought

An alternative type of "higher-order" account of consciousness
suggests that what matters is not higher-order perception but

higher-order thought. David Rosenthal's version is straight-forward:

> Conscious states are simply mental states we are conscious of being in. And, in general, our being conscious of something is just a matter of our having a thought of some sort about it. Accordingly, it is natural to identify a mental state's being conscious with one's having a roughly contemporaneous thought that one is in that mental state.   (1986: 335)

At least that is clear. But is it plausible? Do we really have an actual thought about every single conscious experience? Even when we do have such thoughts, they often come only *after* we have started to have the experience they are about. It's only after experiencing a twinge of toothache that I tend to think about it: the idea that having a thought about it is what made it conscious in the first place is at best surprising. Rosenthal suggests that the thoughts which make mental states conscious need not themselves be conscious. But in that case what reason is there to suppose we are having them at all? No doubt the hypothesis that such thoughts may be unconscious fits the theory; but that hardly makes the theory more acceptable.

To avoid that objection others have suggested "dispositional" accounts. The idea is that a state's being conscious does not require it to be actually thought about by the subject, but only *available* to be thought about. In Peter Carruthers's version of this approach, perceptual contents are passed to two short-term memory stores, C (conscious) and N (non-conscious). The contents of C contribute to the processes of "conceptual thinking", which include higher-order thoughts involving "mind-reading". (The contents of N feed into other processes involved in the control of action.) Carruthers argues that the presence of a mind-reading subsystem has effects on the contents of the short-term memory store C; specifically, that it ensures each experience has a dual content. One part of this content is that such-and-such an experience is taking place (it might be for example *red*); the other part of the content presents how it *seems* (it might be *seems red* or *experience of red*: see Carruthers 2000: 242). He claims that such "dual content" is what ensures that the state has a "feel": is phenomenally conscious (2000: 243f.). I must leave it as an exercise for the reader to examine this approach more closely.

In spite of the attractions of higher-order accounts of phenomenal consciousness, they have trouble dealing with the fact that the following two propositions do not seem to be equivalent:

(a) For an experience to be phenomenally conscious is for there to be *something it is like* to have it.
(b) For an experience to be phenomenally conscious is for the subject *to be aware of* what the experience is like.

Rosenthal, for example, asserts: "When a mental state is conscious, it is not simply that we are conscious of that state; we are conscious of being in that state" (1997: 741). That appears to commit him to the view that (a) is equivalent to (b). But that is by no means obvious, and indeed appears to be mistaken. (For discussion, see Dretske 1993.) Higher-order accounts would be more acceptable if we could legitimately assume that any account of consciousness according to conception (a) must also qualify as an account under conception (b). But it is not clear that being aware of *what* an experience is like is the same as there being *something* it is like to have it. Conception (b) seems more sophisticated than conception (a), in that while (b) requires the subject to have something like appropriate concepts of experience, (a) does not. For that reason conception (b) seems to exclude animals other than ourselves, so that conflating (a) and (b) diminishes the appeal of this approach.

8.7 Review

I believe it is possible to improve on the accounts of consciousness that we have considered so far. In the following sections I will sketch what I think is a promising new approach. It is not new through and through, of course, if only because it owes much to functionalism; and I will only sketch it because space is limited. By way of preparation let us briefly review the accounts we have examined in the course of this and the preceding chapters.

Behaviourists hold that all mental properties are a matter of behaviour and behavioural dispositions. Although this view is most persuasive for the case of intentionality, it is implausible when faced with the phenomena of consciousness. Besides, examples like the pantomime horse and Block's machines make it hard to go along with behaviourism's insistence that the nature of the internal processing doesn't matter (Ch. 5).

Functionalism takes over much that is valuable in behaviourism. However, although in several versions it gives due weight to the organism's relations to the external world, it deliberately makes mental states internal. Some versions take account of the nature of the internal processing and thereby avoid one objection to behaviourism. Also, if we favour a functionalist approach, it seems wise to avoid insisting on definitions (§§3.8, 3.12 and Ch. 6). The value of this approach, then, has to be that in spite of not supplying definitions of individual mental-state terms, it nevertheless helps us to understand their nature. Because there is so much scope for variation, intelligent discussion of functionalism has to attend to the particular details of whichever variety is considered.

Dennett's account – or rather his complex of related accounts – is broadly functionalist as well as broadly behaviourist. What he says repays careful study, although his new metaphors of Multiple Drafts and Joycean machines are disappointing (§§5.7, §6.7, §8.4).

Pure representationalism is a variety of functionalism that is clearly right in this respect at least: that by considering the fact that many if not all mental states *are* representational we can come to understand their nature better. However, by insisting that there is no more to phenomenal character than representational content, it seems to go too far (§8.4).

Accounts which make phenomenal consciousness a matter of higher-order perception have a problem explaining why such perception should necessarily guarantee consciousness, since there is also unconscious perception (§8.5).

Accounts based on the idea of higher-order thought appear, as we have just seen, to conflate two distinct conceptions of consciousness. The result is that they either require too much sophistication of languageless creatures or else imply, implausibly, that such creatures lack feelings (§8.6).

8.8 Preliminaries to a better approach

A useful starting-point for a better approach, I suggest, is the idea of a *deciding system* sketched earlier (§7.8, "Intentionality in other animals"). A deciding system acquires and stores information about its environment: information that it can use. That in turn requires it to have further capacities, notably the capacities to use stored information as a basis for controlling its behaviour; to have goals or objectives; to interpret information; to assess its situation; to choose between alternative courses of action on the basis of stored information. There is a pretty clear sense in which any such system perceives some of the things in its environment. I hope to improve our understanding of phenomenal consciousness in general by focusing on *perceptual* consciousness (§8.1). If we can achieve a reasonably sound understanding of that, we ought to be able to use it as a basis for understanding other forms of phenomenal consciousness, although I will not pursue that project here.

Being a deciding system in the sense explained is necessary for being perceptually conscious, I suggest, but *not* also sufficient. The reason is that there appears to be no contradiction in the idea of a system which acquires its perceptual information rather as people with "blindsight" acquire visual information. Blindsight is an odd phenomenon, where damage to the visual cortex causes partial blindness: there is a blind area either in both right half-fields or else in both left half-fields. Patients insist they see nothing in these "blind fields"; but the peculiar fact is this. When, in a test situation, they are forced to guess which of a small range of objects is being presented in their blind fields, their guesses are significantly better than average. Visual information is being received, therefore, although by comparison with normal vision it is impoverished.

The situation is perhaps rather like that of people with normal vision forced to say what they saw at noon yesterday, or an hour or a minute ago. When forced, we have to recollect or summon up the information; and sometimes it feels like guessing. There is a sharp contrast with the situation when we have our eyes open in normal conditions, when we don't have to guess or summon up the visual information: it strikes us automatically whether we like it or not. In fact it forces itself on us in a way beyond our control (except that we can shut our eyes, block our ears, or hold our noses). An example will help to make these points clearer.

8.9 The rabbitoid

Let us assume for the sake of argument that rabbits are deciding systems in our sense, and that they share the feature of normal perception just noted. Sensory information "forces itself" on them in a way they cannot control, regardless of whether they are made to choose between alternatives (as with blindsight subjects) or otherwise have to "call up" the information (as when we try to remember how things looked ten minutes ago). That seems to fit the actual behaviour of normal rabbits. On those assumptions, if there are lettuces ahead of a rabbit it is able to approach them straight away and start eating. A fox appearing in the distance might not deter the animal from eating; a fox nearby might cause it to run away. The decision is up to it, in contrast with ticks and other creatures whose behaviour is caused directly by reflex circuits.

Now imagine an animal superficially like a rabbit but without that feature. Perceptual information doesn't "force itself" upon this creature – this "rabbitoid" – but is somehow stored away in its memory as it comes in. Perhaps it can call up this information if it does something like what blindsight subjects do when they "guess" what is in their blind fields; or perhaps the information causes alterations in its behaviour that would otherwise not have occurred; or perhaps it somehow "pops up". What it doesn't do is have the immediate impact that incoming perceptual information typically has on normal rabbits and ourselves. Such a creature would obviously be at a great disadvantage compared with a normal rabbit – so much so that it seems highly unlikely that such creatures could have figured in the normal rabbit's evolutionary history. Indeed, being a deciding system may be nomologically sufficient for perceptual consciousness. But even if that is so, the point is that there is a real distinction between a rabbit and a rabbitoid. If that is right, being a deciding system is not sufficient for being a subject of perceptual consciousness.

The question now is: what must be added to the basic package to ensure that the system *is* a subject of perceptual consciousness? It will have to be that feature which I referred to as the perceptual information "forcing itself" upon the organism. Can we say anything more illuminating about it?

8.10 The "direct activity" of incoming perceptual information

I will call this special feature the "direct activity" of incoming perceptual information. I suggest it has two main aspects: *instantaneity* and *priority*. First, instantaneity.

Incoming perceptual information typically equips the subject instantaneously with a whole range of capacities. As I look round the room I become able for example to point to a lot of different red things (books, pens, whatever); to guide my actions accurately if I decide to take a certain book from a shelf; to contrast the sizes, shapes, colours, and many other properties of books and other things. I also become instantly able to recognize many of the things I now see if I come across them again, or see photographs of them. Further, in order for me to be able to exercise any of these instantly acquired and constantly revised and refreshed capacities, nothing else has to happen. I don't have to guess, try to recall, or wait for something to pop up: I am immediately able to act. There is an obvious contrast between the instantaneous acquisition of such capacities on the one hand, and on the other the indirect access to perceptual information that is illustrated by blindsight subjects and the rabbitoid. So much for the "instantaneity" of incoming perceptual information.

Now for "priority". This aspect of direct activity can usefully be grasped from the point of view of evolution. Evidently it's a good thing for an organism to have the basic package: to be able to acquire, store and use perceptual and other information. Even the rabbitoid is better off for having such information (although its ability to use it is rather hit-or-miss), for the information may still help it to achieve its goals. But the real rabbit has a formidable advantage in not only being able to achieve current goals but having the opportunity to revise them in the light of new perceptual information. When the organism's acquisition of perceptual information gives it that opportunity to revise its goals, the information has priority in this special sense. By hypothesis the organism is a deciding system, with the capacity to decide how it will behave on the basis of its information and the capacities to interpret information and to assess its situation. If incoming information gives it the opportunity to revise its goals, therefore, this information must have effects on its processes of interpretation, assessment and decision-making – its "central processes". It must have those effects regardless of whether the information is relevant to its current goals.

Suppose a rabbit is running towards a field of lettuces with the goal of eating them and suddenly spots a fox a little way off. Because visual information about the fox instantaneously has an impact on its central processes it is able to decide to revise its goal: perhaps it chooses to return to its burrow. Contrast the rabbitoid. Even if incoming information is instantly stored away in its memory, and even if this unconscious perception of the fox gives it *some* life-preserving capacities, it doesn't also have this feature of priority: it doesn't give the creature an opportunity to revise its current goals.

My suggestion, then, is that *what it is* for something to be a subject of perceptual consciousness is for it to be a deciding system with the special feature of "direct activity": to be a *deciding system-plus*, as I will say. Being a deciding system-plus, I am suggesting, is not just necessary but sufficient for the perceptual kind of phenomenal consciousness. (As noted earlier, I am not here developing this account so as to cover phenomenal consciousness in general.)

8.11 Replies to objections

Some objections to functionalist approaches were anticipated earlier (§§6.6–6.8); here are one or two others.

Objection A   "The vocabulary you use to describe the basic package and direct activity is not only largely intentional; it is pervaded by implications of consciousness. It's not surprising you seem able to explain consciousness in those terms; but all you have really done is to help yourself to the rich implications of your chosen vocabulary."

Reply A   That is a serious charge, but I don't think it can be sustained. The problematic kind of consciousness is *phenomenal* consciousness, after all. The friends of zombies are typically quite happy to concede that zombies, if they existed, could properly be described in ordinary psychological terms; their claim is only that all those ordinary psychological descriptions could apply to them without their being phenomenally conscious. (See for example Chalmers, who contrasts what he calls the "phenomenal" concept of mind with the "psychological" concept of mind (1996: 11). He claims zombies have full "awareness", which he sees as the "psychological" correlate of phenomenal consciousness.) Of course I think that *if* descriptions specifying the basic package and direct activity apply, then the system is conscious for that reason. But the basis for applying those descriptions in the first place is not that we already know the system is conscious. It is that its behaviour and internal processing entitle us to apply those descriptions *without* first having to decide whether it is conscious. Even if the descriptions are in some way "pervaded by implications of consciousness", we can use them hygienically enough for our purposes here.

Objection B "You're missing the fundamental point. What's essential about phenomenal properties is their feel. In Chalmers's words, what makes states conscious is 'that they have a certain phenomenal feel, and this feel is not something that can be functionally defined away' (1996: 105). Functional states cannot have such feels, at least not essentially. Functional processes could keep churning away in the total absence of phenomenal consciousness. To rub it in: you haven't actually ruled out zombies."

Reply B This objection lumps together three distinct thoughts. One is the assumption that functionalism sets out to "define" phenomenal feel. I agree it seems to be a waste of time to look for such definitions, but I have offered reasons why neither physicalists nor functionalists need to look for them (see §§6.4, 6.5). The aim has to be not to "define" phenomenal feel, but to remove the bafflement we experience when we contemplate it: to make clear how it is that there is such a thing. That is what the account sketched above sets out to do, at least for the perceptual kind of phenomenal consciousness; and the present objection supplies no reason to reject it. A second thought embodied in the objection is that the relevant functional facts could all be there in the absence of phenomenal consciousness; but in this context that is just question-begging: it is like a bald assertion of the zombie possibility. We are left with the main component of the objection: "feels" (or "qualia") are *essential* features of phenomenally conscious states but not of functional states.

That claim is either a further instance of question-begging or a mistake. If the account of perceptual consciousness sketched above is correct, then the performance of certain functions could not possibly occur without there being something it is like for the perceiving subject. That seems to me to imply that "feels" are "essential features" of functional states. If so, the objection begs the question.

Otherwise the objection rests on the mistaken assumption that because not all functional states involve feels, feels are not essential features of functional states. But obviously that is no objection to the claim that certain kinds of functional states – those involved in a deciding system receiving directly active perceptual information – actually *constitute* perceptual consciousness. (See also §6.8, on how functionalists can meet the objection that qualia are "intrinsic".)

Objection C   "You have totally failed to show that a deciding system couldn't receive your 'directly active' perceptual information while remaining unconscious."

Reply C   I think the considerations sketched in §§4.10–4.11 rule out the possibility of zombies. I think they show that the idea that we consist of a fully functioning body plus a set of causally inert non-physical qualia involves a contradiction. On that basis I assume that the present objection cannot help itself to the zombie possibility, or to any other assumption that implies it. The objection had therefore better be only that I have failed to show there is no gap between being a deciding system with directly active perceptual information, and being a subject of perceptual consciousness. Here are some considerations that may help to loosen the grip of the zombie idea, and to show there is no such gap.

Suppose the cat Zoë is a deciding system-plus, and that she sees a sparrow close by and at the same time hears a dog barking further away. Being a deciding system she is able to tell the difference between the dog and the sparrow, and to decide how to behave on the basis of two kinds of incoming information: auditory information about the dog, visual information about the sparrow. But of course her acquisition of these two sorts of information involves two sorts of internal processes. She need not be thinking about them or conceptualizing them as such; but still, in telling the difference between the sight of the bird and the sound of the dog, she is also telling the difference between what are in fact two kinds of internal processes, which have different effects on her central processes of interpretation, assessment and decision (see §8.11. That there are such different internal processes is, I suggest, implied by the "moderate realism" of everyday psychology: §5.9).

Now, when the information about the bird and the dog are coming in with instantaneity and priority, the events constituting Zoë's acquisition of those two sorts of information enable her to modify her current goals. This means they have an immediate impact on her; and by definition it is an impact on her central processes of interpretation, assessment and decision-making. But clearly the two kinds of information must have different kinds of impact: they must strike her differently. I suggest that in that case there is something it is like for her: there is one thing it is like for her to see the sparrow, and something else it is like for her to hear the dog. If that is right she has "qualia" in the relevant sense. Of course she doesn't have qualia in the sense implied by the zombie idea: logically separable and causally inert qualia. I have offered reasons for thinking that conception is incoherent. In reality her having qualia is a matter of internal events performing the functions implied by acquiring perceptual information with instantaneity and priority. The internal events in question constitute her having two kinds of conscious experience.

Objection D   "No matter how much you refine your specification of 'direct activity', there will always be non-standard ways of implementing it which leave the organism without phenomenal consciousness. Block's homunculus-head (or his China-head, where the work is done by the population of a large country such as China) illustrates this point (see §4.9)."

Reply D   The point of this objection is not that I have failed to take account of some relevant functions, although that may well be true. For we saw in §6.6 that functionalists could not easily deny that all relevant functions were indeed performed in the homunculus-head. The objection is that *regardless* of what detailed functions are claimed to provide for phenomenal consciousness, there will always be scope for them to be implemented in ways which defeat such claims. It is one of the standard "absent qualia" objections to functionalism discussed earlier (§6.6).

The force of such objections depends largely on the strength of the intuition that the non-standardly implemented system in question is indeed non-conscious. Block's homunculus-head can certainly seem an unpromising candidate for consciousness, and the China-head perhaps even more so. But what is the source of the trouble? Not, surely, that there are large numbers of individual "units" performing various input–output functions, since that is what happens in our brains. Nor can it be the size of those units: no one would maintain that only very tiny units could possibly provide a basis for phenomenal consciousness. Probably the main factor is that the units are persons, with their own thoughts and feelings. But why should that matter, provided they perform the relevant functions reliably? I know of no non-arbitrary reason.

In any case it seems to me that there is another, much stronger reply to this objection. The objection entails that a system's construction matters even if it makes no relevant functional difference. Hence it entails that there is a *special factor x* which is absolutely necessary for phenomenal consciousness. Now, whether *x* is physical structure, or composition, or spirit-breath, or whatever, is beside the point. For since *x* makes no relevant functional difference, it has no effects on the system's cognitive processes and no effects on its behaviour. That puts it in essentially the same position as the allegedly non-physical, causally inert qualia discussed in Chapter 4. I argued there that the idea of such qualia – and with it the idea of zombies – involves a contradiction. The same goes, I would argue, for the more general idea of factor *x*. But I need not take you through that reasoning again, substituting factor *x* for causally inert non-physical qualia. By now you are in a position to judge for yourself whether it works for the case of factor *x*.

Main points in Chapter 8

1. There are serious difficulties with the main accounts of consciousness on offer today, in spite of their valuable insights (§§8.2–8.6).

2. A fresh approach exploits the idea of a "deciding system", together with that of the "direct activity" of incoming perceptual information (§§8.8–8.11).

Further reading

On consciousness in general see Carruthers (2000), Chalmers (1996), Dennett (1991), Dretske (1995), Kirk (1994), Lycan (1996), Strawson (1994), Tye (1995) and the suggested readings at the end of Block *et al.* (eds) (1997) and in Lycan (ed.) (1990).

Ryle's *The Concept of Mind* (1949) and Wittgenstein's *Philosophical Investigations* (1953) are indispensable. For an introduction to the latter work see Marie McGinn (1997).

McCulloch (1994) offers a good analytically based introduction to Sartre on the mind.

For Dennett's metaphors see Dennett (1991: esp. 101–38, 253–82). For criticism see Carruthers (2000: 280–88).

Versions of pure representationalism are defended in Dretske (1995) and Tye (1995).

On higher-order perception or monitoring see Armstrong (1968) and Lycan (1996, 1997). For criticism see Dretske (1993) and Güzeldere (1997).

On higher-order thought see Carruthers (2000) and Rosenthal (1986, 1997).

9 Conclusion

That ends the main work of this book. I have tried to give you a good idea of the most important problems, theories and arguments enmeshed in the mind–body problem. I have not attempted to mention all the pros and cons of the positions discussed, and I have only touched on, or omitted altogether, a number of topics that are more or less relevant. But one task remains. You may recall that in the Introduction I said the main components of the mind–body problem were intentionality, consciousness, their relations, and the relations between physical and psychological explanations. The first two have each had a chapter to themselves, but not the third. That is partly because the broad and tricky topic of psychological explanation has been with us throughout, partly because it is too broad, and has too many ramifications, to pursue it far in an introductory work. In these last few pages I will draw the main threads together and note some related topics – with suggestions for reading but without any more discussion.

9.1 More about psychological explanation

One fundamental question is: ought we to be realists or eliminativists about the states and properties of everyday psychology? We have noted strong reasons to resist behaviourism (Ch. 5) and eliminativism (§3.9); also some objections to the "industrial strength" intentional realism exemplified by Fodor's LOT hypothesis (Ch. 7). But there are other varieties of psychological realism and anti-realism. We have considered some of these, notably

Davidson's project of "radical interpretation" and his associated views about the nature of intentionality; and Dennett's instrumentalistic approach (§5.6). But the subject is very large. Much more discussion would have been needed before we could sensibly have hoped to go beyond those tentative conclusions.

Another fundamental question is: do psychological explanations force us to appeal to anything beyond the physical? Examination of the arguments suggests there are no good reasons to be dualists, whether substance dualists like Descartes (Ch. 2) or property dualists like Chalmers (Ch. 4). It seems that nothing but the physical is involved in having beliefs, desires and other intentional states, and in being phenomenally conscious. But if that is right it makes the original question more pressing: how are psychological explanations related to physical explanations? If all behaviour is explicable in purely physical terms, how can there be room for psychological explanations? Do they have to be *reduced* to physical explanations?

I sketched an approach to answering those questions in §3.11. Here let me re-emphasise two points. One is that if we are purely physical systems, then the strict implication thesis (SI.1) holds. The other is that in that case any true causal statements, including true statements of psycho-physical causation, are alternative ways of talking about *the same matters of fact* as are already provided for by the conjunction P of purely physical truths. This does not imply, however, that such higher-level truths about causation don't describe real facts, or are otherwise inferior to the truths in P. (If you disagree, you must explain why.)

For further discussions on psychological explanation see Burwood *et al.* (1998), P. M. Churchland (1988), P. S. Churchland (1986), Clark (1989), Davidson (1963, 1974), Dennett (1987), Fodor (1968), Greenwood (ed.) (1991), M. McGinn (1997), Putnam (1985d), Stich (1983) and Wittgenstein (1953).

9.2 More about content

I believe *that it will snow tomorrow*; you may fear the same thing; she sees *that they are having a party*. In Chapter 7 we examined different approaches to explaining what it is for organisms to have such "propositional attitudes"; we also considered a few suggestions about what it is for mental states to have contents. But these topics are much wider than I have made clear so far; and a great deal of work continues to be devoted to them. Apart from Chapters 5 and 7 above, see Burge (1979), Davidson (1974, 1984), Dennett (1969, 1987), Fodor (1987, 1998), Loewer & Rey (eds) (1991), McDowell (1994), C. McGinn (1989), M. McGinn (1997), Putnam (1975b) and Stich (1983).

An interesting problem concerns perceptual experiences. If she sees *that they are having a party*, she surely picks up vastly more information than that bald sentence conveys. She no doubt sees people moving about, and perhaps the colours of their clothes and some of their expressions. Given time and patience she may be able to spell out much of that information. But could she spell out *all* of it? Does she even have suitable *concepts* for specifiying the exact colours of all she sees, for example, or people's exact expressions? In general the richness of experience seems to go beyond what our conceptual equipment can capture.

Those remarks indicate the focus of recent debates over whether or not mental states, especially those involving perceptual experience, have a special type of "non-conceptual" content. Some (for example Peacocke 2001; Tye 1995) claim they do. Others, notably McDowell (1994), maintain that all content is conceptualized or conceptualizable by the subject.

9.3 Externalism

An important aspect of the problem of content, and of psychological explanation generally, concerns relations between mental states and the world. It is easy to assume that what our mental states are depends entirely on what is going on inside us – on "intrinsic" facts about our bodies. Descartes exemplified this assumption when he envisaged the sceptical possibility of a malicious demon providing him with exactly the same mental states as he actually had at the time, while there was no external world at all. In Putnam's phrase, Descartes seems to have assumed "methodological solipsism" (1975b: 220). However, many philosophers today follow Putnam in accepting that the contents of mental states are *not* determined wholly by what's in the thinker's head, but depend on their relations to things outside. If Putnam is right, then, as he puts it, "Cut the pie any way you like, 'meanings' just ain't in the *head*" (*ibid*.: 227). That is *externalism* about intentionality and the contents of mental states. Many philosophers are externalists. For explanations and discussions see, for example, Burge (1979), Fodor (1987), Loewer & Rey (eds) (1991), C. McGinn (1989) and Putnam (1975b).

9.4 Normativity and "the space of reasons"

When discussing Davidson's ideas in §§3.6 and 3.7, we noted some differences between psychological explanations and purely physical ones. However, I said little about the important point that psychological explanations are guided by "the constitutive ideal of rationality" (Davidson 1970: 223). Roughly, the idea is that because we have to treat those we are trying to understand as rational, we have to understand both the contents of their beliefs, desires and other intentional states, and how reasons can justify or fail to justify actions and mental states.

This feature of psychological explanation seems to prevent it from being assimilated to physical explanation. It implies a background of concepts and ways of thinking that contrasts strongly with what might be constructed in terms of physics. To point up this contrast, Wilfrid Sellars coined the expression "the space of reasons" (see 1956: 98f.).

The contrast in question is often associated with "*normativity*". Normativity is an extremely vague notion, however. The starting-point for its use in the present context is that many mental states, such as beliefs, are capable of being correct or incorrect. If physicalism required the correctness involved in normativity to be explained in purely physical terms, then it would be a seemingly impossible project; but we have seen that physicalism does not have to aim so high (§§3.1, 3.11, 3.12, 4.2).

For introductory discussions of normativity see Burwood *et al.* (1998: e.g. 66–70, 146–9). There is much relevant material in McDowell (1985, 1994), where he develops thought-provoking suggestions about the relations between the natural world and Sellars's "space of reasons".

Websites

There are numerous philosophical websites. To trace them you might find the following Limited Area Search Engines for philosophy useful:

http://hippias.evansville.edu/

http://noesis.evansville.edu/

David Chalmers has a very full and well-organized "annotated bibliography of contemporary philosophy of mind" at:

http://www.u.arizona.edu/~chalmers/biblio/

The Stanford Encyclopedia of Philosophy is a free online encyclopedia with many entries already accessible, and more on the way:

http://plato.stanford.edu/

References

Armstrong, D. M. 1968. *A Materialist Theory of the Mind*. London: Routledge & Kegan Paul.

Bechtel, W. & A. Abrahamsen, 1991. *Connectionism and the Mind: An Introduction to Parallel Processing in Networks*. Oxford: Blackwell.

Bickle, J. 1998. *Psychoneural Reduction: The New Wave*. Cambridge, MA: MIT Press.

Block, N. 1978. "Troubles with Functionalism". In *Minnesota Studies in the Philosophy of Science 9*, W. Savage (ed.), 261–325. Minneapolis, MN: University of Minnesota Press. Reprinted in Lycan (ed.) (1990), 444–68.

Block, N. 1980. "Are Absent Qualia Impossible?", *Philosophical Review* **89**: 257–74.

Block, N. (ed.) 1980. *Readings in the Philosophy of Psychology*, vol. 1. London: Methuen.

Block, N. 1981. "Psychologism and Behaviourism", *Philosophical Review* **90**: 5–43.

Block, N. 1995. "On a Confusion about a Function of Consciousness", *Behavioral and Brain Sciences* **18**: 227–47.

Block, N., O. Flanagan, G. Güzeldere (eds) 1997. *The Nature of Consciousness: Philosophical Debates*. Cambridge, MA: MIT Press.

Burge, T. 1979. "Individualism and the Mental". In *Midwest Studies in Philosophy*, vol. 4, P. French *et al.* (eds), 73–121. Minneapolis, MN: University of Minnesota Press.

Burwood, S., P. Gilbert, K. Lennon 1998. *Philosophy of Mind*. London: UCL Press.

Carnap, R. 1938. "Logical Foundations of the Unity of Science". Reprinted in Feigl & Sellars (eds) (1949), 408–23. (Originally published in *International Encyclopedia of Unified Science, I, i.*)

Carruthers, P. 2000. *Phenomenal Consciousness: A Naturalistic Theory*. Cambridge: Cambridge University Press.

Chalmers, D. J. 1996. *The Conscious Mind: In Search of a Fundamental Theory*. Oxford: Oxford University Press.

Chalmers, D. J. 1999. "Materialism and the Metaphysics of Modality", *Philosophy and Phenomenological Research* **59**: 475–96.

Chalmers, D. J. 2002a. "Does Conceivability Entail Possibility?" In *Conceivability and Possibility*, T. Gendler & J. Hawthorne (eds), 145–200. Oxford: Oxford University Press.

Chalmers, D. J. 2002b. "The Content and Epistemology of Phenomenal Belief". In *Consciousness: New Philosophical Perspectives*, Q. Smith & A. Jokic (eds), 220–72. Oxford: Oxford University Press.

Chalmers, D. J. & F. Jackson 2001. "Conceptual Analysis and Reductive Explanation", *Philosophical Review* 110: 315–61.

Churchland, P. M. 1981. "Eliminative Materialism and the Propositional Attitudes", *Journal of Philosophy* 78: 67–90. Reprinted in Lycan (ed.) (1990), 206–23, to which page references apply.

Churchland, P. M. 1985. "Reduction, Qualia, and the Direct Introspection of Brain States", *Journal of Philosophy* 82: 8–28.

Churchland, P. M. 1988. *Matter and Consciousness*, revised edition. Cambridge, MA: MIT Press.

Churchland, P. S. 1986. *Neurophilosophy: Toward a Unified Science of the Mind–Brain*. Cambridge, MA: MIT Press.

Churchland, P. M. & P. S. Churchland 1983. "Stalking the Wild Epistemic Engine", *Noûs* 17: 5–18. Reprinted in Lycan (ed.) (1990), 300–11.

Clark, A. 1989. *Microcognition: Philosophy, Cognitive Science, and Parallel Distributed Processing*. Cambridge MA: MIT Press.

Copeland, J. 1993. *Artificial Intelligence: A Philosophical Introduction*. Oxford: Blackwell.

Davidson, D. 1963. "Actions, Reasons, and Causes", *Journal of Philosophy* 60: 685–700. Reprinted in Davidson (1980).

Davidson, D. 1970. "Mental Events". In *Experience and Theory*, L. Foster & J. W. Swanson (eds), 79–101. London: Duckworth. Reprinted in Davidson (1980), 207–45, to which page references apply.

Davidson, D. 1974. "Belief and the Basis of Meaning", *Synthese* 27: 314–28. Reprinted in Davidson (1984), 141–54, to which page references apply.

Davidson, D. 1980. *Essays on Actions and Events*. Oxford: Clarendon Press.

Davidson, D. C. 1984. *Inquiries into Truth and Interpretation*. Oxford: Clarendon Press.

Dennett, D. C. 1969. *Content and Consciousness*. London: Routledge & Kegan Paul.

Dennett, D. C. 1971. "Intentional Systems", *Journal of Philosophy* 68: 87–106. Reprinted in Dennett (1978a), 3–22.

Dennett, D. C. 1978a. *Brainstorms*. Cambridge MA: MIT Press.

Dennett, D. C. 1978b. "A Cure for the Common Code?" See Dennett (1978a), 90–108.

Dennett, D. C. 1978c. "Artificial Intelligence as Philosophy and as Psychology", in Dennett (1978a), 109–26.

Dennett, D. C. 1987. *The Intentional Stance*. Cambridge, MA: MIT Press.

Dennett, D. C. 1991. *Consciousness Explained*. Boston: Little, Brown.

Dennett, D. C. 1995. "The Unimagined Preposterousness of Zombies", *Journal of Consciousness Studies* 2: 322–6.

Descartes, R. 1968. *Discourse on Method and the Meditations*, F. E. Sutcliffe (trans.). London: Penguin. Page references are to this translation. (The

Discourse was originally published in 1637, the *Meditations* in 1641.)

Descartes, R. 1984–91. *The Philosophical Writings of Descartes*, J. Cottingham, R. Stoothoff, D. Murdoch and A. Kenny (eds and trans.). Cambridge: Cambridge University Press.

Dretske, F. 1993. "Conscious Experience", *Mind* 102: 263–83.

Dretske, F. 1995. *Naturalizing the Mind*. Cambridge, MA: MIT Press.

Feigl, H. & W. Sellars (eds) 1949. *Readings in Philosophical Analysis*. New York: Appleton–Century–Crofts.

Fodor, J. A. 1968. *Psychological Explanation*. New York: Random House.

Fodor, J. A. 1974. "Special Sciences", *Synthese* 28: 77–115. Reprinted in Fodor 1981, 127–45, to which page references apply.

Fodor, J. A. 1975. *The Language of Thought*. New York: Thomas Y. Crowell.

Fodor, J. A. 1981. *Representations: Philosophical Essays on the Foundations of Cognitive Science*. Brighton: Harvester, 127–45, to which page references apply.

Fodor, J. A. 1987. *Psychosemantics: The Problem of Meaning in the Philosophy of Mind*. Cambridge MA: MIT Press.

Fodor, J. A. 1998. *Concepts: Where Cognitive Science Went Wrong*. Oxford: Clarendon Press.

Fodor, J. A. & Z. Pylyshyn 1988. "Connectionism and Cognitive Architecture: A Critical Analysis", *Cognition* 28, 3–71.

Foster, J. 1982. *The Case for Idealism*. London: Routledge & Kegan Paul.

Foster, L. & J. W. Swanson (eds) 1970. *Experience and Theory*. London: Duckworth.

Gendler, T. & J. Hawthorne (eds) 2002. *Conceivability and Possibility*. Oxford: Oxford University Press.

Greenwood, J. D. (ed.) 1991. *The Future of Folk Psychology*. Cambridge: Cambridge University Press.

Güzeldere, G. 1997. "Is Consciousness the Perception of What Passes in One's Own Mind?" See Block *et al.* (eds) (1997), 789–806.

Heil, J. & A. Mele (eds) 1993. *Mental Causation*. Oxford: Clarendon Press.

Hempel, C. 1935. "The Logical Analysis of Psychology". Reprinted in Feigl & Sellars (eds) (1949), 373–84. (Originally published in the *Revue de Synthese*.)

Hill, C. S. 1991. *Sensations: A Defense of Type Materialism*. Cambridge: Cambridge University Press.

Hill, C. S. 1997. "Imaginability, Conceivability, Possibility and the Mind–Body Problem", *Philosophical Studies* 87: 61–85.

Hill, C. S. & B. P. McLaughlin 1999. "There are Fewer Things in Reality Than Are Dreamt of in Chalmers's Philosophy", *Philosophy and Phenomenological Research* 59: 446–54.

Hofstadter, D. R. 1981. "Prelude . . . Ant Fugue". See Hofstadter & Dennett (1981), 149–91.

Hofstadter, D. R. & D. C. Dennett (eds) 1981. *The Mind's I*. New York: Basic Books.

Horgan, T. 1984. "Jackson on Physical Information and Qualia", *Philosophical Quarterly* 34: 147–53.

Horgan, T. & J. Tienson 1996. *Connectionism and the Philosophy of Psychology*. Cambridge, MA: MIT Press.

Jackson, F. 1982. "Epiphenomenal Qualia", *Philosophical Quarterly* 32: 127–36. Reprinted in Lycan (ed.) (1990), 469–77.

Kenny, A. 1968. *Descartes: A Study of his Philosophy*. New York: Random House.

Kenny, A. 1973. *Wittgenstein*. London: Penguin.

Kim, J. 1989. "The Myth of Nonreductive Materialism". See Kim (1993), 265–84.

Kim, J. 1993. *Supervenience and Mind*. Cambridge: Cambridge University Press.

Kirk, R. 1974. "Zombies v. Materialists", *Proceedings of the Aristotelian Society*, supp. vol. 48: 135–42.

Kirk, R. 1981. "Goodbye to Transposed Qualia", *Proceedings of the Aristotelian Society* 82: 33–44.

Kirk, R. 1986. "Mental Machinery and Gödel", *Synthese* 66: 437–52.

Kirk, R. 1994. *Raw Feeling: A Philosophical Account of the Essence of Consciousness*. Oxford: Clarendon Press.

Kirk, R. 1996. "Strict Implication, Supervenience, and Physicalism", *Australasian Journal of Philosophy* 74: 244–56.

Kirk, R. 1999. "Why There Couldn't Be Zombies", *Proceedings of the Aristotelian Society*, supp. vol. 73: 1–16.

Kirk, R. 2001. "Nonreductive Physicalism and Strict Implication", *Australasian Journal of Philosophy* 79: 545–53.

Kripke, S. 1972. *Naming and Necessity*. Oxford: Blackwell.

Leibniz, G. H. 1973. *Philosophical Writings*, G. H. R. Parkinson (ed.). London: Dent.

LePore, E. (ed.) 1986. *Truth and Interpretation: Perspectives on the Philosophy of Donald Davidson*. Oxford: Blackwell.

Levine, J. 2001. *Purple Haze: the Puzzle of Consciousness*. Oxford: Oxford University Press.

Lewis, D. 1966. "An Argument for the Identity Theory", *Journal of Philosophy* 63: 17–25.

Lewis, D. 1972. "Psychophysical and Theoretical Identifications", *Journal of Philosophy* 50: 249–58.

Lewis, D. 1983. "Mad Pain and Martian Pain". In *Philosophical Papers, vol. I*, D. Lewis, 122–32. New York: Oxford University Press.

Lewis, D. 1994. "Reduction of Mind". In *A Companion to the Philosophy of Mind*, S. Guttenplan (ed.), 412–31. Oxford: Blackwell.

Loewer, B. & G. Rey (eds) 1991. *Meaning in Mind: Fodor and his Critics*. Oxford: Blackwell.

Lucas, J. R. 1961. "Minds, Machines and Gödel", *Philosophy* 36: 112–27. Reprinted in *Minds and Machines*, A. R. Anderson (ed.), 43–59. (Englewood Cliffs, NJ: Prentice-Hall, 1964) to which page references apply.

Lycan, W. G. (ed.) 1990. *Mind and Cognition: A Reader*. Oxford: Blackwell.

Lycan, W. G. 1996. *Consciousness and Experience*. Cambridge, MA: MIT Press.

Lycan, W. G. 1997. "Consciousness as Internal Monitoring". See Block *et al.* (1997), 756–71.

McCulloch, G. 1994. *Using Sartre*. London: Routledge.

McDowell, J. 1985. "Functionalism and Anomalous Monism". In *Actions and Events: Perspectives on the Philosophy of Donald Davidson*, E. LePore & B. P. McLaughlin (eds), 387–98. Oxford: Blackwell.

McDowell, J. 1994. *Mind and World*. Cambridge, MA: Harvard University Press.

McFarland, D. (ed.) 1987. *The Oxford Companion to Animal Behaviour*. Oxford: Oxford University Press.

McGinn, C. 1982. *The Character of Mind*. Oxford: Oxford University Press.

McGinn, C. 1989. *Mental Content*. Oxford: Blackwell.

McGinn, C. 1991. *The Problem of Consciousness*. Oxford: Blackwell.

McGinn, M. 1997. *Wittgenstein and the* Philosophical Investigations. London: Routledge.

Millikan, R. 1986. "Thoughts without Laws", *Philosophical Review* **95**: 47–80.

Nagel, E. 1961.*The Structure of Science*. New York: Harcourt Brace.

Nagel, T. 1974. "What Is It Like to Be a Bat?", *Philosophical Review* **83**: 435–50. Reprinted in *Mortal Questions*, T. Nagel, 165–80 (Cambridge: Cambridge University Press, 1979).

Nagel, T. 1986. *The View from Nowhere*. Oxford: Oxford University Press.

Nagel, T. 1998. "Conceiving the Impossible and the Mind–Body Problem", *Philosophy* **73**: 337–52.

Nemirow, L. 1980. Review of T. Nagel's *Mortal Questions*, *Philosophical Review* **89**: 473–77.

Papineau, D. 2002. *Thinking about Consciousness*. Oxford: Clarendon Press.

Peacocke, C. 2001. "Does Perception Have a Nonconceptual Content?", *Journal of Philosophy* **98**: 239–64.

Putnam, H. 1960. "Minds and Machines". In *Dimensions of Mind*, S. Hook (ed.), 139–64. New York: New York University Press. Reprinted in Putnam (1975a), 362–85.

Putnam, H. 1967. "The Mental Life of Some Machines". In *Intentionality, Minds and Perception*, H. Castaneda (ed.), 177–200. Detroit, MI: Wayne State University Press. Reprinted in Putnam (1975a), 408–28.

Putnam, H. 1975a. *Mind, Language and Reality: Philosophical Papers vol. ii.* Cambridge: Cambridge University Press.

Putnam, H. 1975b. "The Meaning of 'Meaning'". See Putnam (1975a), 215–71.

Putnam, H. 1975c. "Philosophy and Our Mental Life". See Putnam (1975a), 291–303.

Putnam, H. 1975d. "The Nature of Mental States". See Putnam (1975a), 429–40.

Putnam, H. 1981. *Reason, Truth and History*. Cambridge: Cambridge University Press.

Quine, W. V. 1960. *Word and Object*. Cambridge, MA: MIT Press.

Quine, W. V. 1981. *Theories and Things*. Cambridge, MA: Harvard University Press.

Ramsey, W., S. P. Stich, J. Garon 1991. "Connectionism, Eliminativism, and the Future of Folk Psychology". See Ramsey *et al.* (eds), 199–228.

Ramsey, W., S. P. Stich, D. E. Rumelhart (eds) 1991. *Philosophy and Connectionist Theory*. Hillsdale, NJ: Erlbaum.

Rosenthal, D. M. 1986. "Two Concepts of Consciousness", *Philosophical Studies* 49: 329–59.

Rosenthal, D. M. 1997. "A Theory of Consciousness". See Block *et al.* (1997), 729–53.

Ryle, G. 1949. *The Concept of Mind*. London: Hutchinson.

Sartre, J.-P. 1958. *Being and Nothingness: A Phenomenological Essay on Ontology*, H. E. Barnes (trans.). London: Methuen. Originally published as *L'Être et le Néant* (Paris: Gallimard, 1943).

Searle, J. R., 1980. "Minds, Brains, and Programs", *Behavioral and Brain Sciences* 3: 417–24. Reprinted in Hofstadter and Dennett (1981), 353–73, to which page references apply.

Searle, J. R. 1992. *The Rediscovery of the Mind*. Cambridge, MA: MIT Press.

Sellars, W. 1956. "Empiricism and the Philosophy of Mind". In *Minnesota Studies in the Philosophy of Science 1*, H. Feigl & M. Scriven (eds), 253–329. Minneapolis, MN: University of Minnesota Press.

Shoemaker, S. 1975. "Functionalism and Qualia", *Philosophical Studies* 27: 291–315.

Shoemaker, S. 1981a. "Absent Qualia are Impossible – A Reply to Block", *Philosophical Review* 90: 581–99.

Shoemaker, S. 1981b. "The Inverted Spectrum", *Journal of Philosophy* 79: 357–81.

Smart, J. J. C. 1959. "Sensations and Brain Processes", *Philosophical Review* 68: 160–72. Reprinted, slightly revised, in *Materialism and the Mind–Body Problem*, D. Rosenthal (ed.) (Englewood Cliffs, NJ: Prentice-Hall, 1971): 53–66.

Smith, P. & O. R. Jones 1986. *The Philosophy of Mind: An Introduction*. Cambridge: Cambridge University Press.

Stich, S. P. 1983. *From Folk Psychology to Cognitive Science: The Case Against Belief*. Cambridge, MA: MIT Press.

Strawson, G. 1994. *Mental Reality*. Cambridge, MA: MIT Press.

Turing, A. M. 1950. "Computing Machinery and Intelligence", *Mind* 59: 433–60. Reprinted in Hofstadter and Dennett (1981), 53–67, to which page references apply.

Tye, M. 1986. "The Subjective Qualities of Experience", *Mind* 85: 1–17.

Tye, M. 1995. *Ten Problems of Consciousness: A Representational Theory of the Phenomenal Mind*. Cambridge, MA: MIT Press.

Wilkes, K. V. 1978. *Physicalism*. London: Routledge & Kegan Paul.

Wilkinson, R. 2000. *Minds and Bodies: An Introduction with Readings*. London: Routledge.

Wittgenstein, L. 1953. *Philosophical Investigations*, G. E. M. Anscombe (trans.). Oxford: Blackwell.

Index